The Essential Elements
Copyright © 2024
Kendall Peterson
All rights reserved.

No part of this book may be reproduced, stored in a retrieval system, or transmitted in any form or by any means—electronic, mechanical, photocopying, recording, or otherwise—without the prior written permission of the author, except in the case of brief quotations embodied in critical articles and reviews.

For information, contact:
Kendall Peterson

ISBN: 9781300801184

First Edition
Printed in the United States of America

Published by: Kendall Peterson

The information in this book is for educational purposes only. The author has made every effort to ensure the accuracy of the information herein; however, the author assumes no responsibility for errors or omissions.

CONTENTS

ACKNOWLEDGEMENTS		5
INTRODUCTION		9
CHAPTER 1:	UNVEILING THE ESSENTIAL ELEMENTS	18
CHAPTER 2:	PURPOSE – CHARTING THE COURSE	36
CHAPTER 3:	TEAM – THE RIGHT PEOPLE IN THE RIGHT ROLES	54
CHAPTER 4:	SYSTEMS – BUILDING A FOUNDATION FOR CONSISTENCY	70
CHAPTER 5:	MEASUREMENT – NAVIGATING WITH DATA	86
CHAPTER 6:	RELATIONSHIPS – CULTIVATING CONNECTIONS	102
CHAPTER 7:	COMMUNICATION – THE GLUE OF THE ORGANIZATION	116

CHAPTER 8:	INNOVATION – STAYING AHEAD OF THE CURVE	130
CHAPTER 9:	BRINGING THE 7 ELEMENTS TOGETHER	142
CHAPTER 10:	CALL TO ACTION	156

CONCLUSION 173

ACKNOWLEDGEMENTS

No book is ever written alone. While my name may be on the cover, this work is the culmination of countless influences, encouragements, and inspirations—each leaving a unique mark on every page. I owe an enormous debt of gratitude to so many people who have been part of this journey.

First and foremost, I want to acknowledge my incredible wife, Arlene. Your unwavering support, encouragement, and love have been the foundation on which I have built so much of my life. You have always seen the best in me, even on days when I couldn't see it myself. You've been my partner, my confidant, and my greatest source of strength. I am forever grateful for your patience, your faith in me, and your belief that there is always something greater ahead. This book would not exist without your enduring encouragement and gentle (yet persistent) nudges to keep pushing forward.

To my kids—thank you for always grounding me in what truly matters. Your joy, curiosity, and love have been constant reminders that success is nothing without the relationships that give it meaning. Watching you grow has been my greatest privilege, and everything I do is, in some way, for you.

And to my wife's family, who welcomed me into their lives and treated me as one of their own—thank you for your kindness, love, and continuous support. Your encouragement and belief in me have meant more than you'll ever know. I am deeply grateful to be part of this family, and your support has been a pillar throughout this journey.

I also want to thank the "angels" in my life, some of whom might not even realize the role they played. Jack Nelson, Tom McDermott, David Daniels, Carman Wenkoff, and Hector Hernandez — each of you showed up at pivotal moments, offering support, advice, or just the right words at exactly the right time. Your impact has been profound, and I often wonder how different the path would have been without you. You reminded me that sometimes the people who cross our paths—even if briefly—can have a lasting influence that extends far beyond the moment.

And above all, I want to express my deepest gratitude to my Lord and Savior, Jesus Christ. Although I spent the first 42 years of my life ignoring Him, His love, grace, and sacrifice have shaped everything I am today. Thank You for Your unending patience and for never giving up on me, even when I wasn't looking in Your direction. Your example of love, humility, and purpose is a guiding light that I strive to follow, even if imperfectly. Every good thing in my life is a testament to Your goodness, and every success is a reflection of Your blessings.

May this work honor all of you.

INTRODUCTION

It's the rats I remember the most. Not the sewer-dwelling monsters from horror movies with glowing red eyes, just ordinary dumpster rats. But to a 15-year-old kid navigating homelessness alone, they might as well have been something out of a nightmare. At first, every rustle in the shadows sent my heart racing. I'd yell, throw whatever I could find—half-eaten sandwiches, discarded shoes, even a perfectly good cassette tape of '80s southern rock (regretted that one).

Over time, though, something strange happened. Maybe it was the way they looked at me with those beady eyes, or maybe I just got tired of wasting food. We reached an unspoken agreement. They were just like me, after all—searching for food, shelter, and a sense of place in a world that didn't seem to care. We became unlikely roommates behind the dumpster at Jack's Diner, a spot where luxury was as absent as hope felt at the time. And there I was, sharing scraps of fries with these unlikely companions, spending hours contemplating how I'd ended up there.

Now, you might be wondering if this is really a business book or if you picked up a gritty memoir by mistake. But to understand how a homeless teenager in the back lot of a diner found his way to helping businesses thrive, we need to go back— back to where it all began, with my mother, the original entrepreneur in my life.

My mother was born toward the end of the Great Depression to a hardworking, blue-collar family in the heartlands of Iowa. If resilience and tenacity were Olympic sports, she'd have more gold medals than Michael Phelps. She was pretty, with a smile that could light up a room and a spirit that seemed to beg for life's adventures.

She was a secretary who worked at a military base and my father caught her eye. He was a Marine—disciplined, steadfast, and sporting a uniform that seemed tailor-made for a recruiting poster. With his square jaw and a posture so straight you'd think he had a steel rod for a spine, he was the embodiment of order in a world that often felt chaotic.

Perhaps it was his unwavering sense of duty that caught her eye, or maybe it was the way he carried himself with a confidence that suggested he could handle anything life threw at him. She was no stranger to hardship, and maybe that's what drew them together—a mutual understanding that life is a battlefield, and it's better to face it with someone by your side.

But dreams have a funny way of throwing in plot twists worthy of a soap opera. When my parents divorced, it wasn't just a splitting of assets—which, to be fair, didn't extend much beyond a broken toaster a collection of vinyl records warped by the summer heat. It was a seismic upheaval that shook the foundations of everything we knew. Financial stability went out the window, followed closely by any semblance of normalcy.

At the time, Mom was only making $17,000 per year, so she quickly had to become a one-woman circus act, juggling odd jobs and side hustles to pay the bills. She tried multilevel marketing schemes, signed up with startups promising the world, and even launched her own ventures.

Despite her relentless efforts and an optimism that could have powered a small city, we teetered on the edge of financial instability. Living with her was like residing in a house built on quicksand—every step threatened to sink us deeper. Bills piled up, lights and water routinely disconnected, and the phrase "just a minor setback" was thrown around regularly.

By the time I hit the ripe old age of 15, the house of cards had collapsed. Home became a fluid concept, more of a theoretical construct than a physical place. And that's how I found myself at Jack's Diner, a greasy spoon that made no pretense of being anything else. The dumpster out back became my "home," and the rats—well, oddly enough, in my mind they were the only ones who wouldn't judge me for where I'd ended up.

It's astonishing the kind of clarity that can emerge when you're at your lowest point—both literally and metaphorically rummaging through garbage. Amidst the aroma of day-old meatloaf and the dulcet tones of traffic and distant sirens, I pondered life's big questions: Why do hot dogs come in packs of ten but buns in packs of eight? Is there intelligent life out there, and if so, could they loan me five bucks? But most importantly: "How do I never let this happen again?"

That question was the spark that ignited an inferno within me, a relentless desire to understand the mechanics of success and failure. I became obsessed, not unlike how a dog becomes fixated on chasing its own tail, except my chase involved devouring every piece of information I could find about business, leadership, and organizational dynamics in the local library.

Fast forward a few years, and you'll find me buried under mountains of business books, case studies, and enough highlight markers to paint a rainbow. I wasn't just reading about Fortune 500 companies; I was dissecting them with the enthusiasm of a kid taking apart a radio to see how it works, except with fewer electrical shocks.

Over the years, I've studied over 2,200 different businesses. Yes, you read that correctly—two thousand two hundred businesses. I've had the privilege of learning from great business leaders and coaches—icons like Tony Robbins, who could probably convince a fish to climb a tree, and Zig Ziglar, whose sales techniques could sell sand in the desert and throw in a complimentary cactus. I immersed myself in success programs like *The Seven Habits of Highly Effective People*. I delved into Norton & Kaplan's *The Balanced Scorecard*. And of course, I couldn't ignore *Start with Why* by Simon Sinek.

Early in my career, I was fortunate to be part of an organization that didn't just pay lip service to quality improvement but embraced it. We're talking Six Sigma, Total Quality Management (TQM), and tons of process improvement. I was part of a team that won the Edward Deming Prize for Quality and the Malcolm Baldrige National Quality Award. If there were accolades for attending an obscene number of meetings about process flowcharts, my mantelpiece would be dangerously overloaded.

For more than 15 years, I've steered my consulting practice through partnerships with over 300 organizations. In that time, I've seen it all: from the downright absurd—like the CEO convinced that success was only possible if he clocked 16-hour days—to the truly inspiring, where teams moved with the seamless coordination of a symphony in perfect harmony, just without the black-tie attire.

But here's the twist in the narrative: Despite all this experience, all these accolades that look impressive on a LinkedIn profile or when trying to win an argument at a dinner party, I don't claim to know everything. In fact, the more I peel back the layers of business complexity, the more I realize that knowledge is like Swiss cheese—the more you have, the more holes you find.

Through it all, one truth became clear though: **Success isn't random. It follows a formula.**

Certain principles consistently lead to success. They're not hidden in ancient scrolls guarded by mystical monks atop some fog-shrouded mountain. They're not the exclusive domain of geniuses who drink soy lattes and use "ideate" as a verb. They're common sense—so profoundly straightforward that they're often overlooked.

I've distilled these principles into what I call **The Essential Elements**. Think of them as the fundamental building blocks that every successful organization uses, whether they're flipping burgers or launching rockets. These Elements—Purpose, Team, Systems, Measurement,

Relationships, Communication, and Innovation—are like the essential elements in chemistry. On their own, they're powerful, but when combined, they create transformative reactions that elevate an organization to greatness. Miss one, and it's like trying to bake a cake without flour—you might end up with something resembling food, but no one's going back for seconds.

This book is an invitation—a challenge, even—to explore these seven elements and assess how they play out in your own organization. We'll dive deep into each one, sharing stories that range from laugh-out-loud funny to "I can't believe they thought that was a good idea" levels of absurdity. We'll look at companies that got it spectacularly right, turning modest investments into empires, and others that serve as cautionary tales, like the business equivalent of a "Don't Do This at Home" warning.

So, if you're ready to learn, buckle up. Whether you're an executive, an entrepreneur, or just someone who wants to understand the mechanics of success, there's something here for you. Success isn't a mystery reserved for a select few. It's accessible to anyone willing to understand and apply these principles. And more than anything, it's achievable.

Remember, success isn't some elusive mystery. It's a formula—a set of steps that are accessible to anyone willing to learn. And it starts with understanding the elements that make a difference.

So grab a cup of coffee and let's dive into *The Essential Elements*. You might just find the tools you need to turn even the darkest of beginnings into launching pads for success.

CHAPTER 1:

UNVEILING THE ESSENTIAL ELEMENTS

If you're still with me after the introduction, that means a few things: first, you survived my opening story and are at least somewhat curious about these "7 Essential Elements". Second, you're probably the type of person who wants to build something great—whether it's a team, a business, or an entirely new vision for your organization.

So, here's the question: why 7 elements? Why not 5 or 10? The truth is, I didn't stumble upon this framework overnight. It took years of experience, thousands of case studies, and more than a few hard lessons. The Essential Elements are not just concepts—they're the tangible building blocks that create success. When one of these elements is missing, an organization might function, but it won't thrive.

Before we dive into each of these elements, let's take a moment to understand what they are and why they matter. Think of them as the foundational pillars that hold up the entire structure of your organization.

UNDERSTANDING THE SEVEN ELEMENTS

Here's a quick overview of The Essential Elements, which we'll break down in detail throughout the book:

1. Purpose
2. Team
3. Systems

4. Measurement
5. Relationships
6. Communication
7. Innovation

While you might recognize these words, they represent far more than simple business jargon. Each one is a strategic component that, when properly developed, becomes a catalyst for sustainable growth and resilience. Let's explore what each of these elements really means and how they contribute to creating a high-performing organization.

1. PURPOSE: THE 'WHY' BEHIND EVERYTHING

Purpose is the driving force of your organization. It's the why behind every action, every strategy, and every decision. Companies that lack a clear purpose often find themselves drifting, chasing profits without direction. But those with a compelling purpose are like a ship with a strong rudder—they can navigate any storm and still stay on course.

Imagine a company like *Patagonia*, the outdoor apparel brand. They aren't just selling jackets and hiking boots; their purpose is to build the best product while causing no unnecessary harm to the environment and using business to inspire solutions to the environmental crisis. This clarity of purpose isn't just good for marketing—it's a powerful tool that attracts loyal customers, motivates employees, and aligns every decision they make.

But what happens when a company doesn't have a clear purpose? Think of *Sears*, which was once a retail giant. As the years passed, their purpose became unclear, shifting from appliances to insurance and everything in between. The lack of a consistent direction led to confusion, loss of market position, and eventually bankruptcy. Their demise wasn't just about the rise of online shopping; it was about losing sight of who they were.

A well-defined purpose:

- **Aligns the Organization**: Provides a shared understanding of what the organization is striving for.
- **Inspires Commitment**: Motivates employees to go the extra mile, because they're working for something greater than themselves.
- **Differentiates Your Brand**: Sets you apart in a crowded marketplace, making your company memorable and meaningful.

When an organization's purpose is clear and compelling, it doesn't just attract talent—it galvanizes people around a shared mission, turning strategy into reality.

2. TEAM: THE RIGHT PEOPLE IN THE RIGHT ROLES

Your Team is the living, breathing heart of your organization. Having the right people in the right seats can make or break your business. But building a great team isn't just about hiring smart people—it's about creating a culture where diverse talents can thrive, contribute, and grow.

The best example of a team firing on all cylinders is *Apple* during Steve Jobs' return in the late 1990s. Jobs didn't just hire talented engineers—he cultivated a team that shared his vision for elegance, simplicity, and user experience. They weren't just building computers; they were creating tools to change the world. This alignment, combined with diverse skill sets and a shared passion, transformed Apple from a struggling company into a global powerhouse.

Contrast this with the infamous case of *Enron*. They hired some of the brightest minds in finance and energy—but the team lacked a shared purpose and moral compass. The result? An organization that prioritized personal gain over integrity, leading to one of the biggest corporate collapses in history. The lesson is clear: without the right culture and values, even the most talented team can turn toxic.

Key aspects of building a strong team include:

- **Recruitment**: Attract individuals who align with your organization's core values.

- **Development**: Invest in training and career growth opportunities.
- **Engagement**: Create an environment where team members feel valued and motivated.

Having the right people in the right roles doesn't just lead to better performance—it becomes a powerful force multiplier that accelerates success.

3. SYSTEMS: THE BACKBONE OF EFFICIENCY

Systems are the nuts and bolts of your organization—the processes, procedures, and structures that ensure things run smoothly. Without effective systems, even the best team will struggle to get things done. A system is what enables an organization to be consistent, repeatable, and scalable.

Take *McDonald's* as an example. It's not just about burgers and fries—it's about a system that allows them to deliver a consistent experience in thousands of locations across the globe. Their processes are so refined that a teenager with no work experience can step into a McDonald's and start contributing productively on day one. Systems create a backbone of predictability and quality, which allows the organization to scale massively.

Now think about *Blockbuster*. At its height, Blockbuster had the market dominance and brand recognition to define an entire industry. But their internal systems were rigid and slow to change. As Netflix embraced new technologies and business models, Blockbuster clung to outdated processes, unable to adapt quickly enough. The result? A once-dominant brand became a relic of the past, unable to compete in a world that moved faster than its systems could support.

Effective systems should:

- **Streamline Operations**: Simplify tasks and eliminate unnecessary steps.
- **Enhance Quality**: Ensure products or services meet consistent standards.
- **Support Scalability**: Enable the organization to grow without sacrificing performance.

When systems are working, they become the invisible engine that powers your organization's success.

4. MEASUREMENT: KNOWING WHERE YOU STAND

Measurement is about more than just numbers—it's about understanding what's working, what's not, and what to do next. Think of it like being a pilot in a cockpit. Your organization, like an aircraft, has many moving parts that need to function in harmony. The pilot doesn't just glance at random dials and hope for the best. Every instrument on the dashboard—altitude, airspeed, fuel levels, navigation—

tells a specific story. Without that information, even a seasoned pilot would be flying blind, unable to make the split-second decisions that keep the plane on course.

In the business world, your metrics are those gauges. They let you know when you're on track, when you're veering off course, and when you're heading straight into turbulence. But just as a pilot can't afford to focus solely on airspeed while ignoring fuel levels, leaders must be careful not to get fixated on a single metric at the expense of others.

Consider *Amazon*, where metrics aren't just tracked—they drive every aspect of decision-making. Jeff Bezos famously said, "If you can't measure it, you can't improve it." At Amazon, data points like customer satisfaction, delivery speed, and inventory turnover aren't just collected—they form the very backbone of how the company operates. This relentless focus on measurement has allowed Amazon to refine its operations, optimize processes, and anticipate market needs, keeping them consistently ahead of the competition.

Now look at *Kodak*, a company that was once a giant in the world of photography. They measured their film sales meticulously, watched profits roll in, and felt confident about their market position. But they missed one critical metric: the rapid shift toward digital photography. They were staring intently at one gauge—film sales—while the real crisis was unfolding in a different part of the dashboard. By the time they recognized the trend, it was too late. Their failure wasn't due to a lack of data—it was focusing on the wrong data. Like a pilot staring at the altimeter while the fuel gauge flashes empty, Kodak was tracking metrics that no longer mattered.

Effective measurement requires:

- **Choosing the Right Gauges**: Identify the key metrics that truly indicate the health and direction of your organization.
- **Reading the Data Accurately**: Understand what each number is telling you—whether it's signaling a course correction or a green light to push forward.
- **Making Informed Decisions**: Use the data to navigate, adjust, and stay aligned with your long-term strategy.

Measurement is your compass, your altimeter, and your fuel gauge all rolled into one. When used correctly, it's what turns guesswork into precision, giving you the confidence to navigate your organization through both smooth skies and stormy weather.

5. RELATIONSHIPS: THE LIFEBLOOD OF YOUR ORGANIZATION

Relationships are the true lifeblood of any organization. They go far beyond just transactions or contracts—they are the deep, trust-based connections that allow your business to thrive and grow over time. When relationships are strong, they build loyalty, foster collaboration, and create a foundation of mutual support that can withstand the inevitable challenges every business will face.

The importance of building and maintaining strong relationships is perfectly illustrated by the success of Southwest Airlines. Unlike many of its competitors, Southwest has consistently prioritized relationships—both internally, with its employees, and externally, with its customers. From the start, founder Herb Kelleher emphasized that the way you treat your employees will ultimately reflect in how they treat your customers. This philosophy became a guiding principle for the company's culture, leading to a fiercely loyal customer base and an employee turnover rate far below the industry average. Even in times of crisis, like the post-9/11 airline industry slump, Southwest's commitment to relationships kept it strong while other airlines struggled.

But what happens when an organization neglects relationships? Consider the downfall of Wells Fargo. For years, Wells Fargo was known for its reputation as a trusted financial institution, built on a foundation of solid customer relationships. That trust was shattered when it was revealed that employees, pressured by unrealistic sales goals, had created millions of fake customer accounts. The fallout was catastrophic. Not only did it result in billions in fines and a tanking stock price, but it severely damaged the bank's relationship with its customers. The brand has yet to fully recover, showing how quickly a lack of genuine relationship-building can undermine decades of hard-earned goodwill.

Building solid relationships involves:

- **Customer Engagement**: Understanding and meeting customer needs consistently and with empathy.
- **Supplier Partnerships**: Collaborating for mutual benefit, ensuring that every partnership is rooted in shared goals and respect.
- **Community Involvement**: Contributing positively to the broader community, creating a network of support that extends beyond business transactions.

When relationships are strong, they act as a buffer against competition and a springboard for future growth. Customers who feel valued will stick with you through ups and downs, and partners who trust you will be willing to collaborate on opportunities that could take your business to the next level.

6. COMMUNICATION: THE GLUE THAT HOLDS IT ALL TOGETHER

Communication is the glue that binds your entire organization together. It's how your purpose is expressed, how your team aligns, and how your strategy comes to life. Without clear communication, even the best-laid plans can crumble. Think of it as the nervous system of your business—ensuring that every part of the organization is connected, informed, and able to respond to changes in the environment.

One company that truly understands the power of communication is *Netflix*. In a groundbreaking internal document titled The Netflix Culture Deck, the company laid out its expectations for transparency, open dialogue, and direct feedback. This deck became legendary in Silicon Valley, influencing not just Netflix's own operations but the entire tech industry's approach to company culture. Netflix's emphasis on "freedom and responsibility" means that employees are encouraged to speak up, share ideas, and even challenge leadership if it's in the interest of making the company better. This openness has fostered a culture of innovation, agility, and trust, propelling Netflix from a mail-order DVD service to a global entertainment powerhouse.

Now consider a case where poor communication led to disastrous results: the *Volkswagen* emissions scandal. For years, Volkswagen engineers were aware that the company's diesel cars did not meet emissions standards, but the communication channels within the company were so fractured that this information never made it to the top in a transparent manner. Instead of addressing the problem head-on, the company resorted to deceit, ultimately installing software to cheat emissions tests. When the truth came out, it wasn't just the deception that hurt Volkswagen—it was the company's lack of open, honest communication that enabled such a large-scale scandal to go undetected. The result? A shattered reputation, billions in fines, and a long road to recovery.

Effective communication strategies include:

- **Transparency**: Sharing information openly to build trust and reduce misunderstandings.
- **Clarity**: Conveying messages in a straightforward and understandable manner, ensuring everyone is on the same page.
- **Feedback Mechanisms**: Creating channels for employees, partners, and customers to share their thoughts and ideas, making them feel heard and valued.

When communication is prioritized, it doesn't just prevent problems—it fosters a sense of unity and shared purpose. People feel connected, engaged, and empowered to contribute meaningfully to the organization's goals.

7. INNOVATION: STAYING AHEAD OF THE CURVE

When we think of innovation, it's easy to imagine disruptive technologies or radical new products. But true innovation is more than just groundbreaking ideas—it's a mindset of continuous improvement and problem-solving that keeps your organization relevant and agile. Innovation isn't just about being first; it's about being better.

One company that embodies this philosophy is *Toyota*, with its principle of kaizen, or continuous improvement. Toyota's approach wasn't to reinvent car manufacturing overnight but to refine every process incrementally, every day. Workers on the assembly line were encouraged to pull the "Andon Cord" to halt production if they spotted an issue—an action that seems counterproductive at first but led to a dramatic reduction in defects and waste over time. This focus on solving small problems continuously transformed Toyota into a global leader in quality and efficiency.

Now, contrast this with *BlackBerry*. At its peak, BlackBerry was the gold standard for smartphones, but it failed to innovate beyond its original product. The company was overly focused on defending its existing model rather than adapting to a rapidly changing market. They missed the opportunity to solve new problems that the shift toward touchscreens and app ecosystems presented. By the time BlackBerry tried to catch up, it was too late—the market had moved on.

Effective innovation is built on:

- **Solving Problems Proactively**: Identifying and fixing issues before they become critical.
- **Continuous Improvement**: Making small changes that compound into big gains.
- **Creating a Culture of Experimentation**: Encouraging every team member to look for ways to improve, no matter how small.

Innovation isn't just about creating something new—it's about making what you have better. Companies that embed problem-solving and continuous improvement into their culture are the ones that will stay ahead, no matter how the landscape shifts.

THE ROLE OF EACH FACTOR IN BUSINESS SUCCESS

Each of these seven elements is critical on its own, but their real power is in how they complement each other. Think of it like a finely tuned orchestra: every instrument (or in this case, every factor) has a role to play, but the magic happens when they come together in perfect harmony. When all seven elements are firing together, the result is an organization that's more resilient, more agile, and ultimately more successful.

For example:

- A strong Purpose inspires your Team, which in turn, leverages Systems to work efficiently.
- Effective Communication ensures that Innovation is shared, understood, and acted upon.
- Robust Measurement identifies opportunities to strengthen Relationships and maximize the impact of new initiatives.

The interplay between these elements is what sets high-performing organizations apart from the rest. It's not just about having each element in place—it's about making sure they're aligned and working together toward a common goal.

By mastering all seven elements, you'll not only build a more effective organization—you'll build one that can thrive in the face of change, adapt to new challenges, and create lasting value for everyone involved.

In the chapters that follow, we won't just define each element. We'll dive deep into what they look like in practice, sharing both positive examples of organizations that exemplified the power of these elements and cautionary tales of those that fell short. You'll get practical guidance on how to apply each element to your own business, plus actionable steps to take whether you're leading a team, running your own startup, or just starting to shape your own leadership path.

And remember, all roads lead to action. After we unpack each element, we'll bring it all together with a comprehensive Call to Action chapter to help you translate what you've learned into real, tangible outcomes—no matter what role you play in your organization.

So turn the page, and let's start at the beginning—with Purpose. Because without Purpose, even the best strategies and the most talented teams can find themselves adrift. Ready to chart a course?

Let's get started.

CHAPTER 2:

PURPOSE - CHARTING THE COURSE

Imagine setting sail on a vast ocean without a compass, map, or even a vague idea of your destination. Sure, the open sea is beautiful, but without direction, you're more likely to end up reenacting scenes from *Cast Away* than discovering new lands. In the business world, **Purpose** is your compass—it's what keeps you on course amidst storms, sirens, and the occasional tempting detour to a metaphorical ice cream shop.

In this chapter, we'll delve into the essence of Purpose, exploring why it's not just corporate jargon but the heartbeat of any thriving organization. So hoist the sails, grab your spyglass, and let's navigate these waters together.

DEFINING PURPOSE

The Importance of Setting a Clear Direction

Let's face it: wandering aimlessly is only fun if you're in a rom-com montage or have an unlimited supply of snacks. In business, ambiguity is the enemy. A clear **Purpose** provides the direction that aligns your team's efforts and resources. It's the North Star that guides decisions, big and small, ensuring everyone is paddling in the same direction rather than spinning in circles like a confused duck.

Consider Purpose as the answer to the existential question every organization must face: *"Why do we exist?"* Spoiler alert: "To make money" isn't enough to inspire greatness. Profit is a result, not a purpose. Your Purpose should reflect a deeper mission that resonates with both your team and your customers.

Crafting a Compelling Purpose That Motivates and Aligns
Creating a Purpose statement isn't about stringing together impressive words like "synergy," "leverage," and "paradigm." It's about articulating a mission that genuinely reflects your organization's values and aspirations. It should be:

- **Authentic**: True to who you are and what you believe.
- **Inspirational**: Capable of igniting passion and commitment.
- **Clear**: Easy to understand and remember (if it requires footnotes, try again).

For example, let's say you're running a coffee shop. A Purpose like "To caffeinate the masses" is serviceable but lacks pizzazz. However, "To create moments of joy and connection over the world's finest coffee" adds a touch of magic. It elevates the mundane to the meaningful.

WHY PURPOSE MATTERS

Provides Specific Focus for Daily Activities
With a well-defined Purpose, daily tasks become more than just items on a to-do list; they become steps toward fulfilling a mission. Employees understand how their roles contribute to the bigger picture, which enhances

motivation and engagement. Instead of feeling like cogs in a machine, they see themselves as integral parts of a meaningful endeavor.

Imagine an employee named Lisa in your coffee shop. Without a clear Purpose, making lattes might feel routine. But knowing she's part of "creating moments of joy and connection" transforms her job into an opportunity to make someone's day brighter.

That extra sprinkle of cinnamon on a cappuccino? It's not just garnish; it's a manifestation of Purpose.

Secures Agreement and Buy-In from All Stakeholders
A compelling Purpose unites everyone involved with your organization—employees, customers, suppliers, and even that grumpy landlord who insists the rent is due on the first of every month (how rude). When stakeholders resonate with your Purpose, they're more likely to support your endeavors, forgive occasional missteps, and become advocates for your brand.

Purpose acts like a magnet, attracting like-minded individuals and organizations. It creates a shared sense of identity and commitment, fostering loyalty and collaboration.

STRATEGIC PLANNING

The Role of Strategic Planning in Realizing the Purpose

If Purpose is your compass, **Strategic Planning** is your map. It's the process of defining the path to achieve your mission, setting goals, and determining the actions needed to get there. Without a plan, even the most inspiring Purpose can become a pipe dream.

Strategic Planning involves:

- **Setting Objectives**: Defining clear, measurable goals that align with your Purpose.
- **Allocating Resources**: Determining where to invest time, money, and talent.
- **Developing Tactics**: Outlining the specific steps and initiatives required.

Think of it as plotting your journey on the high seas. You need to know which ports to visit, how much provisions you'll need, and how to avoid those pesky pirates (or in business terms, competitors).

Acknowledging the Variety of Strategic Planning Approaches

There's no one-size-fits-all method for Strategic Planning. Some organizations prefer a top-down approach, while others embrace collaborative planning involving all levels of the team. Popular frameworks include SWOT analysis

(Strengths, Weaknesses, Opportunities, Threats), OKRs (Objectives and Key Results), and the Balanced Scorecard.

The key is to choose an approach that fits your organization's culture and needs. Whether you're a tech startup in a trendy loft or a family-owned bakery, the plan should be as unique as your grandma's secret recipe.

BENEFITS OF EFFECTIVE PURPOSE SETTING

Building Consensus Around Goals and Priorities

When everyone understands and believes in the Purpose, aligning on goals becomes much smoother. It reduces the likelihood of internal conflicts and turf wars over resources. Instead of departments acting like rival siblings fighting over the last slice of pizza, they collaborate to serve the greater mission.

Guiding Resource Allocation and Operational Planning

A clear Purpose helps prioritize initiatives and investments. It answers questions like:

- Where should we focus our efforts?
- Which projects align best with our mission?
- How do we balance short-term needs with long-term objectives?

By filtering decisions through the lens of Purpose, you ensure that resources are directed toward activities that advance your mission, rather than being wasted on shiny objects that distract and derail.

Evaluating Organizational Performance

Purpose provides a benchmark against which to measure success. It's not just about hitting sales targets or reducing costs; it's about assessing how well you're fulfilling your mission. This broader perspective encourages a more holistic view of performance, encompassing customer satisfaction, employee engagement, and social impact.

Stimulating Positive Change

A compelling Purpose can be a catalyst for transformation. It challenges the status quo and inspires innovation. When everyone is committed to a higher mission, they're more likely to embrace change, take calculated risks, and pursue continuous improvement.

PRACTICAL APPLICATION - PURPOSE

Steps to Develop and Communicate a Powerful Purpose

- **Clarify the Mission and Vision**: Begin by ensuring that your Mission and Vision Statements are well-defined and aligned. The Mission articulates your organization's core purpose and daily focus, while the Vision defines your long-term aspirations and success criteria.

- **Identify Core Values as Guiding Principles**: Establish the non-negotiable values that guide behaviors and decision-making. These should be clear, succinct, and reflective of who you are as an organization, anchoring your strategy and fostering alignment in times of change.

- **Engage Stakeholders for Strategic Alignment**: Don't do this yourself. Involve key team members, partners, and clients to capture diverse perspectives and foster buy-in. Their feedback will help ensure the Purpose resonates, is realistic, and aligns with your long-term strategic goals.

- **Conduct a SWOT Analysis to Inform Purpose**: Use a structured SWOT Analysis to evaluate internal strengths and weaknesses, and identify external opportunities and threats. This analysis should inform your Purpose, ensuring it addresses your strategic realities and aspirations.

- **Communicate as a Strategic Driver**: Communicate the finalized Purpose across multiple channels, reinforcing its role as the foundation of your strategy. Link it explicitly to your strategy map, tactical plans, and prioritization efforts so that it drives focus and action at every level.

- **Integrate into Strategy, Operations, and Culture**: Embed the Purpose into every aspect of your strategic planning process—use it to inform strategic objectives, guide tactical planning, and shape organizational culture. Ensure it's reflected in how progress is measured, obstacles are addressed, and success is defined.

Ensuring the Purpose Permeates the Organizational Culture

Purpose shouldn't be a plaque on the wall that everyone ignores like that motivational poster in the break room. It needs to be lived and breathed:

- **Leadership Modeling**: Leaders must embody the Purpose in actions and decisions.

- **Storytelling**: Share stories that highlight the Purpose in action. Celebrate successes and learn from setbacks.
- **Hiring Practices**: Recruit individuals who align with the Purpose. Cultural fit is as important as skills.
- **Continuous Reinforcement**: Regularly revisit and discuss the Purpose to keep it fresh and relevant.

POSITIVE USE CASE - PURPOSE

An Organization That Transformed Its Fortunes by Uniting Around a Clear Purpose: NASA and the Apollo Program

In the early 1960s, the United States was locked in a fierce space race with the Soviet Union. The launch of Sputnik and the first human orbit by Yuri Gagarin had put the Soviets ahead. The U.S. needed a unifying Purpose to rally the nation and reclaim technological leadership.

The Vision: President Kennedy's Challenge

On May 25, 1961, President John F. Kennedy addressed a joint session of Congress, declaring:

"I believe that this nation should commit itself to achieving the goal, before this decade is out, of landing a man on the Moon and returning him safely to the Earth."

This bold Purpose was clear, measurable, and inspirational. It wasn't just about space exploration; it was a statement of technological prowess and national ambition.

| THE TRANSFORMATION OF NASA

Alignment and Focus:

- Unified Mission: NASA, which had been working on various projects, now had a singular Purpose.

Every program, resource, and team member aligned toward the Moon landing goal.
- Strategic Planning: Detailed plans were developed, including the Mercury, Gemini, and Apollo programs, each building on the previous to achieve the ultimate objective.

Mobilization of Resources:

- Investment: The U.S. government allocated substantial funding, recognizing that achieving this Purpose required significant resources.
- Talent Acquisition: NASA attracted some of the brightest minds—scientists, engineers, and astronauts—all motivated by the shared mission.

Cultural Impact:

- National Pride: The Purpose extended beyond NASA, inspiring universities, industries, and the public.
- Innovation: The challenges of the mission spurred technological advancements in computing, materials science, and telecommunications.

The Success: Apollo 11

On July 20, 1969, Apollo 11 landed on the Moon. Astronaut Neil Armstrong took his famous "one small step for man, one giant leap for mankind." The mission achieved President Kennedy's Purpose within the decade, as promised.

Impact:

- Technological Leadership: The U.S. established itself as a leader in space exploration.
- Legacy of Innovation: The technologies developed had far-reaching effects, leading to advancements in various industries.
- Organizational Excellence: NASA became a model for how a clear Purpose, combined with strategic planning and resource alignment, can lead to monumental achievements.

The Apollo Program exemplifies how a compelling Purpose can unify an organization (and even a nation), drive innovation, and achieve what once seemed impossible. By uniting around President Kennedy's vision, NASA transformed ambiguity into focused success, leaving a legacy that continues to inspire.

NEGATIVE USE CASE - PURPOSE

The Downfall of a Giant Without a Clear Purpose: Yahoo!
In the bustling early days of the internet, Yahoo! emerged as one of the most recognizable brands. Launched in 1994 by Jerry Yang and David Filo, Yahoo! started as a simple directory of websites but quickly expanded into a multifaceted internet portal offering email, news, finance, and a myriad of other services. At its peak in the early 2000s, Yahoo! was a powerhouse, competing fiercely with emerging giants like Google and Amazon.

The Challenge: Undefined and Shifting Purpose
Despite its early success, Yahoo! struggled to maintain a clear and consistent Purpose. The company's mission seemed to oscillate between being a comprehensive internet portal, a search engine competitor, and a media conglomerate. This lack of focus created internal confusion and diluted the brand's identity.

Key Issues:

- Lack of Clear Vision: Yahoo! never fully committed to a singular Purpose. Attempts to juggle multiple objectives led to strategic misalignments.

- Frequent Leadership Changes: The revolving door of CEOs brought varying visions and priorities, preventing the establishment of a stable, long-term strategy.

- Diversification Without Synergy: Expanding into diverse areas like original content creation and acquisitions (e.g., Tumblr, GeoCities) without ensuring they aligned with a central Purpose.

The Missteps: Inconsistent Strategies and Missed Opportunities

Yahoo!'s inability to define and adhere to a clear Purpose manifested in several critical missteps:

1. Failure to Compete in Search:
    - Missed Focus: While Google honed in on becoming the best search engine, Yahoo! treated search as just one of many services, failing to innovate and optimize it effectively.
    - Inefficient Investments: Resources were spread thin across various projects, leading to inadequate development of the search platform.

2. Overambitious Acquisitions:
    - Tumblr Acquisition (2013): Yahoo! acquired Tumblr for $1.1 billion, aiming to capture the younger demographic. However, integration challenges and mismatched business models

prevented Tumblr from thriving under Yahoo!'s umbrella.
- GeoCities Acquisition: Attempting to expand its social presence, Yahoo! bought GeoCities but struggled to revitalize the platform in an era moving towards more modern social networks.

3. Inconsistent Product Development:
   - Varied Offerings: From email services to online advertising and media content, Yahoo!'s product lines lacked cohesion, making it difficult to establish expertise or leadership in any single area.
   - User Experience Issues: The sprawling array of services led to a cluttered user interface, frustrating users who sought simplicity and efficiency.

The Impact: Decline and Loss of Market Leadership

Yahoo!'s failure to maintain a clear Purpose had dire consequences:

- **Loss of Market Share**: As Google dominated the search engine market and Facebook took over social networking, Yahoo!'s relevance waned.

- **Financial Struggles**: Inconsistent revenue streams and failed investments led to financial instability.

Yahoo!'s stock price plummeted, and the company struggled to attract and retain advertisers.

- **Reputation Damage**: High-profile missteps and leadership turmoil eroded trust among users, investors, and partners.

- **Ultimate Sale**: In 2017, Verizon acquired Yahoo!'s core internet business for approximately $4.48 billion, a fraction of its former valuation, marking the end of Yahoo! as an independent entity.

Yahoo!'s decline serves as a stark reminder of the importance of a clear and unwavering Purpose. Without a defined mission, organizations can become directionless, making it challenging to allocate resources effectively, innovate meaningfully, and maintain a strong brand identity. Yahoo!'s ambitious diversification and inconsistent strategies diluted its impact, allowing more focused competitors to seize leadership roles in key areas.

CONCLUSION: SETTING SAIL WITH PURPOSE

Defining and embracing your organization's Purpose is not a trivial exercise; it's the foundation upon which all else is built. It's the beacon that guides your team through calm seas and stormy weather alike.

By crafting a compelling Purpose, you:

- Inspire and Align Your Team: Giving meaning to their work beyond paychecks.
- Clarify Decision-Making: Providing a consistent framework for choices and priorities.
- Connect with Customers: Resonating on a deeper level that fosters loyalty.

The success of NASA's Apollo Program illustrates the transformative power of a clear Purpose, while Kodak's struggles highlight the risks of failing to adapt one's Purpose to a changing environment.

Remember, Purpose isn't static. It can and should evolve as your organization grows and the world changes. Regularly revisit and refine it to ensure it remains relevant and impactful.

So, hoist your sails, set your compass, and embark on your journey with a clear Purpose. The destination? A successful, fulfilling voyage where everyone knows why they're on board and eagerly contributes to the adventure.

In the next chapter, we'll explore the crew that will help you navigate these waters: your Team. After all, even the best captain can't sail alone. So turn the page, and let's meet the people who will bring your Purpose to life.

CHAPTER 3:

TEAM – THE RIGHT PEOPLE IN THE RIGHT ROLES

BY KENDALL PETERSON

Picture this: You're assembling a puzzle, but half the pieces are from a different set, and some are missing entirely. Frustrating, right? That's what it's like trying to build a successful organization without the right team in place. In the grand tapestry of business, your **Team** is the thread that weaves everything together. Without the right people in the right roles, even the most brilliant strategy can unravel faster than a cheap sweater.

In this chapter, we'll explore the importance of building a team that's not just competent but also aligned with your organization's core values. So grab your magnifying glass and detective hat; it's time to solve the mystery of assembling a dream team.

UNDERSTANDING THE TEAM FACTOR

The Significance of Having the Right People in the Right Seats

Jim Collins, in his seminal work *Good to Great*, emphasized the importance of getting "the right people on the bus." But it's not just about filling seats; it's about ensuring each person is in **the right seat**. Imagine a symphony where the violinist and percussionist swap places. The result would be a cacophony rather than harmony.

Having the right people in the right roles ensures that:

- **Skills Match Responsibilities**: Talents are effectively utilized.
- **Efficiency Increases**: Tasks are performed competently, reducing errors.
- **Morale Improves**: People are more satisfied when their roles align with their strengths.

The Impact of Shared Core Values on Organizational Cohesion

Shared core values act like the glue that holds your team together. They foster a sense of belonging and purpose. When team members align with the organization's values, they are more likely to:

- **Collaborate Effectively**: Understanding and trust flourish.
- **Make Aligned Decisions**: Choices reflect the organization's ethos.
- **Stay Committed**: Employee retention improves as people feel connected.

Consider core values as the DNA of your organization. They define who you are and influence how your team behaves internally and externally.

| WHY TEAM MATTERS

Employees as the Lifeblood of the Organization
Let's debunk a myth: companies aren't faceless entities; they're living organisms comprised of people. Your employees are the heartbeat, pumping vitality into every project, interaction, and innovation. Without them, your grand vision remains a mere idea scribbled on a napkin.

Employees influence:

- **Customer Experience**: Frontline staff shape customer perceptions.
- **Innovation**: Diverse teams bring fresh ideas and perspectives.
- **Culture**: Daily interactions create the workplace environment.

Aligning Individual Strengths with Organizational Needs
Maximizing your team's potential isn't about squeezing every ounce of effort from them; it's about aligning their unique strengths with the organization's needs.

Benefits include:

- **Enhanced Performance**: People excel when working in areas that leverage their talents.
- **Increased Engagement**: Employees are more invested when they feel their contributions matter.

- **Reduced Turnover**: Satisfied employees are less likely to seek opportunities elsewhere.

Think of it as a Venn diagram where individual passions and skills intersect with organizational goals—the sweet spot where magic happens.

RIGHT PEOPLE, RIGHT SEATS

Defining "Right People" Through Core Values Alignment
Identifying the "right people" starts with your core values. They serve as a litmus test to determine cultural fit.

Ask yourself:

- Do they share our mission and vision?
- Do their personal values align with ours?
- Will they enhance our culture or disrupt it?

It's not about cloning personalities but about finding individuals who resonate with your organization's heartbeat.

Assessing Capabilities, Understanding, and Desire
Once you've identified cultural fit, assess whether they are in the "right seat."

Consider the following:

- **Capabilities**: Do they have the skills and experience required?
- **Understanding**: Do they grasp the role's expectations and how it contributes to the bigger picture?
- **Desire**: Do they genuinely want to perform this role?

A "yes" to all three suggests you've found the right person for the right seat.

PRACTICAL APPLICATION - TEAM

Methods for Evaluating and Placing Talent

1. **Comprehensive Interviews**: Go beyond standard questions to understand candidates' values and motivations.
2. **Skill Assessments**: Use tests or simulations to gauge abilities relevant to the role.
3. **Personality Profiles**: Tools like the Myers-Briggs Type Indicator or DISC assessment can provide insights into work styles and team compatibility.
4. **Cultural Fit Interviews**: Involve team members in the hiring process to assess alignment.
5. **Trial Periods**: Offer probationary periods to evaluate performance in real-world scenarios.

Developing a Culture That Attracts and Retains Top Performers

- **Offer Growth Opportunities**: Invest in professional development and career advancement paths.
- **Recognize and Reward**: Acknowledge contributions through praise, promotions, or incentives.
- **Foster Inclusivity**: Create an environment where diverse perspectives are valued.
- **Communicate Transparently**: Keep lines of communication open to build trust.

- **Promote Work-Life Balance**: Support employees' well-being to prevent burnout.

By cultivating such a culture, you become a magnet for top talent who not only excel in their roles but also become ambassadors for your brand.

POSITIVE USE CASE - TEAM

A Success Story of Organizational Turnaround Through Strategic Hiring: Southwest Airlines

When it comes to putting the right people in the right roles, Southwest Airlines is a shining example. Founded in 1967, Southwest has grown to become one of the largest and most respected airlines in the United States, not just because of its low fares but largely due to its people-centric culture.

| ENHANCING PERFORMANCE BY REALIGNING ROLES

The Challenge:
In the highly competitive airline industry, many companies focus primarily on cost-cutting and operational efficiency, often at the expense of employee morale. Southwest took a different approach. They recognized that to provide exceptional customer service and maintain profitability, they needed a team that was not only skilled but also deeply aligned with the company's core values of warmth, friendliness, and a Warrior Spirit.

The Strategy:

- **Hiring for Attitude and Cultural Fit:**
  Southwest prioritized hiring individuals who embodied their core values, even if they lacked

industry experience. They believed skills could be taught, but attitude and alignment with the company's culture were paramount.

- **Empowering Employees:**
Employees were encouraged to be themselves and make decisions that would enhance the customer experience. This empowerment fostered a sense of ownership and pride in their work.

- **Investing in Employee Development:**
Southwest offered extensive training and development opportunities, ensuring that employees had the capabilities and understanding to excel in their roles.

The Impact:

- **Exceptional Customer Service:**
Passengers often rave about Southwest's friendly and helpful staff. Flight attendants are known for their humorous safety announcements and willingness to go the extra mile.

- **High Employee Satisfaction:**
Southwest consistently ranks as one of the best places to work. Employee turnover is significantly lower than the industry average.

- **Financial Success:**
  The company's focus on people translated into profitability. Southwest has enjoyed decades of consistent profits, a rarity in the airline industry.

By strategically hiring and placing the right people in the right roles, Southwest Airlines created a strong, cohesive team that drives both customer satisfaction and financial performance. Their success demonstrates the power of aligning individual strengths and values with organizational needs.

NEGATIVE USE CASE - TEAM

The Pitfalls of Ignoring Cultural Fit and Role Suitability: Enron Corporation

On the flip side, the tragic downfall of Enron Corporation serves as a cautionary tale about the dangers of ignoring cultural fit and ethical alignment within a team.

The Cost of High Turnover and Employee Disengagement

The Challenge:

Enron, once a darling of Wall Street and a symbol of innovation in the energy sector, collapsed in 2001 due to massive accounting fraud. While the primary issue was unethical leadership, underlying problems with team alignment and culture played a significant role.

The Missteps:

- **Toxic Culture:**
  Enron fostered a highly competitive and cutthroat environment. Employees were encouraged to outperform peers at any cost, leading to unethical behavior.

- **Wrong People in Wrong Roles:**
  Promotions and rewards were often based on short-term revenue generation rather than long-

term value or ethical considerations. This placed individuals in leadership roles who lacked integrity and a commitment to the company's core responsibilities.

- **Lack of Ethical Alignment:**
The company's core values were overshadowed by greed and ambition. There was little emphasis on honesty, transparency, or stakeholder responsibility.

The Impact:

- **Employee Disengagement:**
Many employees felt pressured to engage in unethical practices or risk termination. This led to low morale and a lack of trust within the organization.

- **High Turnover:**
Talented individuals who did not agree with the company's practices left, resulting in a brain drain and further weakening of ethical standards.

- **Collapse and Legal Consequences:**
When the fraudulent activities were exposed, Enron filed for bankruptcy. Thousands of employees lost their jobs and retirement savings. Top executives faced legal action, and the company's reputation was irreparably damaged.

Enron's disregard for cultural fit and ethical alignment in team roles contributed to its downfall. By prioritizing short-term gains and ignoring the importance of having the right people in the right seats, the company created an environment ripe for misconduct. This negative use case highlights the critical need for integrity and alignment in building a sustainable organization.

CONCLUSION: ASSEMBLING YOUR ALL-STAR TEAM

Building the right team is akin to casting a hit movie. You need the right actors in the right roles, delivering performances that resonate with the audience. When everyone is aligned and performing at their best, the result is a blockbuster.

Key Takeaways:

- **Prioritize Cultural Fit:**
  As Southwest Airlines demonstrated, hiring individuals who align with your core values creates a cohesive and motivated team.

- **Align Strengths with Roles:**
  Employees excel when their skills and passions match their responsibilities. Invest in understanding your team's unique talents.

- **Foster an Ethical Culture:**
  Avoid the pitfalls seen in Enron by embedding integrity and ethical behavior into your organizational fabric.

- **Invest in Your People:**
  Provide opportunities for growth and recognize contributions. Your employees are your greatest asset.

- **Be Willing to Make Tough Decisions:**
  Sometimes, parting ways with individuals who do not align with your values is necessary for the greater good.

Remember, your team is more than just a collection of employees; they're the lifeblood of your organization. Treat them as such, and they'll propel your company to new heights.

As we navigate to the next chapter, we'll explore the systems that support your team—ensuring consistency, efficiency, and scalability. After all, even the best team needs a solid foundation to build upon. So, turn the page, and let's delve into the world of Systems.

CHAPTER 4:

SYSTEMS – BUILDING A FOUNDATION FOR CONSISTENCY

BY KENDALL PETERSON

Imagine trying to bake your favorite cake without a recipe. You might remember most of the ingredients, but chances are you'll forget the baking powder or misjudge the oven temperature, resulting in a culinary catastrophe. In the business world, **Systems** are your recipes—they provide the instructions and standards needed to produce consistent, high-quality results. Without them, you're left with guesswork, variability, and a whole lot of burnt cakes.

In this chapter, we'll explore the critical role that Systems play in building a strong organizational foundation. We'll examine how well-designed systems can empower your team, enhance efficiency, and drive continuous improvement. And, as promised, we'll delve into real-world examples that highlight both the triumphs and pitfalls of system implementation.

So, preheat your intellectual ovens, and let's get cooking!

DEFINING SYSTEMS

The Importance of Documented and Followed Procedures
At its core, a **System** is a set of processes or procedures that dictate how tasks are performed within an organization. Documenting these procedures ensures that everyone knows the "how" behind their responsibilities, reducing ambiguity and reliance on memory.

Why Documentation Matters:

- **Consistency:** Provides a uniform approach to tasks, leading to predictable outcomes.
- **Training Aid:** Serves as a valuable resource for onboarding new employees.
- **Accountability:** Establishes clear expectations and standards for performance.

Imagine a world-class orchestra without sheet music. Each musician might be talented, but without a common script, their performance would be chaotic. Similarly, documented systems align your team's efforts toward a harmonious outcome.

ESTABLISHING STANDARDS FOR ACCEPTABLE PERFORMANCE

Systems define what "good" looks like. By setting standards, you create benchmarks for quality, efficiency, and effectiveness. These standards enable you to measure performance objectively and identify areas for improvement.

Key Elements of Effective Standards:

- **Clarity:** Easy to understand and interpret.
- **Relevance:** Directly related to organizational goals.

- **Achievability:** Realistic and attainable with available resources.

Standards act like the rules of a game. Without them, players wouldn't know how to score, and referees couldn't enforce fair play.

WHY SYSTEMS MATTER

Identifying and Rectifying Deviations

With systems in place, deviations from the standard process become apparent. This visibility allows you to address issues proactively before they escalate into significant problems.

Benefits of Detecting Deviations:

- **Quality Control:** Ensures products or services meet customer expectations.
- **Risk Mitigation:** Reduces the likelihood of errors and accidents.
- **Efficiency Gains:** Identifies bottlenecks and unnecessary steps.

Think of systems as the guardrails on a winding road—they keep you on track and prevent you from veering off into dangerous territory.

Serving as a Baseline for Continuous Improvement
Systems provide a foundation upon which you can build and enhance your operations. By analyzing existing processes, you can identify opportunities for optimization.

Continuous Improvement Cycle:

1. **Document:** Capture the current process.
2. **Measure:** Evaluate performance against standards.
3. **Analyze:** Identify gaps and root causes.
4. **Improve:** Implement changes to enhance the system.
5. **Monitor:** Track the impact and adjust as needed.

This cycle, often associated with methodologies like Six Sigma and Lean, fosters a culture of excellence and adaptability.

GOOD SYSTEMS VS. GOOD EXECUTION

The Interplay Between System Design and Execution Quality
Having a well-designed system is essential, but it's only half the battle. Execution—the way your team implements the system—is equally critical.

Scenarios:

- **Good System, Poor Execution:** Even the best processes fail if not followed correctly.

- **Poor System, Good Execution:** Talented teams may compensate temporarily, but inefficiencies persist.
- **Good System, Good Execution:** The ideal combination leading to optimal performance.
- **Poor System, Poor Execution:** A recipe for disaster.

The synergy between system design and execution determines the overall effectiveness of your operations.

ADDRESSING SCENARIOS OF BAD SYSTEMS AND POOR EXECUTION

When problems arise, it's essential to diagnose whether the issue stems from the system, execution, or both.

Steps to Address Issues:

1. **Assess the System:** Is it well-designed, documented, and accessible?
2. **Evaluate Execution:** Are team members trained and equipped to follow the system?
3. **Gather Feedback:** Engage employees to understand challenges and obstacles.
4. **Implement Solutions:** Revise the system, enhance training, or address cultural barriers as needed.

By systematically addressing both elements, you can realign your organization toward success.

PRACTICAL APPLICATION - SYSTEMS

Steps to Document and Implement Effective Systems

1. **Identify Key Processes:** Focus on critical operations that impact quality, safety, or customer satisfaction.
2. **Map the Process:** Visualize each step using flowcharts or diagrams.
3. **Engage Stakeholders:** Involve those who perform the tasks daily to ensure accuracy and buy-in.
4. **Document Procedures:** Create clear, concise instructions, including necessary tools and resources.
5. **Review and Test:** Validate the system by piloting it and making adjustments based on feedback.
6. **Train the Team:** Provide comprehensive training to ensure understanding and competence.
7. **Monitor and Update:** Regularly review the system to incorporate improvements and adapt to changes.

Engaging Employees in System Development

Involving your team in creating and refining systems has multiple benefits:

- **Enhanced Buy-In:** People are more likely to embrace processes they helped develop.

- **Improved Accuracy:** Frontline employees offer practical insights into what works and what doesn't.
- **Empowerment:** Fosters a sense of ownership and accountability.

Encourage open dialogue, solicit suggestions, and recognize contributions to build a collaborative environment.

POSITIVE USE CASE - SYSTEMS

How Streamlined Systems Led to Increased Efficiency: McDonald's

When it comes to systems and consistency, **McDonald's** is a global powerhouse. Serving millions of customers daily across over 100 countries, McDonald's success hinges on its ability to deliver uniform quality and service regardless of location.

THE POWER OF THE "SPEEDEE SERVICE SYSTEM"

Background:
In the 1940s, the McDonald brothers, Richard and Maurice, revolutionized the restaurant industry by introducing the "Speedee Service System." This system applied assembly-line principles to food preparation, emphasizing efficiency and consistency.

Key Elements:

- **Standardized Procedures:** Every item on the menu had a specific preparation process, down to the number of pickles on a burger.
- **Specialized Roles:** Employees were assigned specific tasks (e.g., grilling, assembling, cashiering), optimizing productivity.

- **Equipment Optimization:** Custom-designed kitchen layouts minimized movement and reduced preparation time.

EMPLOYEE EMPOWERMENT THROUGH CLEAR GUIDELINES

- **Training and Development:**
  - **Hamburger University:** Established in 1961, this training facility educates employees and franchisees on McDonald's systems, quality standards, and management practices.
  - **Operational Manuals:** Comprehensive guides detail every aspect of restaurant operations.

- **Impact on Employees:**
  - **Clarity:** Staff know exactly what is expected of them, reducing confusion and errors.
  - **Efficiency:** Well-defined roles and procedures streamline workflows.
  - **Opportunity for Advancement:** Mastery of systems can lead to career growth within the company.

- **Results and Impact**
  - **Consistency:** Customers receive the same experience whether they're in Tokyo, Toronto, or Tulsa.

- o **Efficiency:** Streamlined operations reduce costs and increase throughput.
- o **Scalability:** The ability to replicate systems enabled rapid global expansion.

McDonald's demonstrates how well-designed and executed systems empower employees, enhance efficiency, and deliver consistent value to customers.

NEGATIVE USE CASE - SYSTEMS

THE CHAOS RESULTING FROM UNDOCUMENTED PROCEDURES: FYRE FESTIVAL

In 2017, the world witnessed a spectacular event management failure known as the **Fyre Festival**. Marketed as a luxurious music festival on a private island in the Bahamas, it promised attendees gourmet food, upscale accommodations, and performances by top artists. Instead, it became synonymous with poor planning and lack of systems.

LACK OF PROPER SYSTEMS AND DOCUMENTATION

Planning Failures:

- **No Documented Processes:** There was no formal project plan outlining tasks, timelines, or responsibilities.
- **Inadequate Vendor Management:** Contracts and agreements with suppliers were haphazard, leading to confusion and unmet obligations.
- **Poor Communication:** Information was not effectively shared among team members, leading to conflicting actions and decisions.

Execution Shortcomings:

- **Insufficient Infrastructure:** Basic necessities like housing, sanitation, and medical services were not adequately arranged.
- **Last-Minute Changes:** Constant shifts in plans without proper documentation exacerbated chaos.

CUSTOMER DISSATISFACTION DUE TO INCONSISTENCY

Attendee Experience:

- **Accommodation Disaster:** Luxury villas turned out to be disaster relief tents with soaked mattresses.
- **Food Fiasco:** Gourmet meals were replaced with soggy cheese sandwiches in styrofoam containers.
- **Event Cancellation:** Performances were canceled, and the festival was ultimately called off after guests had arrived.

Consequences:

- **Legal Action:** Attendees filed lawsuits for fraud and breach of contract.
- **Reputational Damage:** The organizers faced public outrage and became subjects of documentaries highlighting the debacle.

- **Financial Losses:** Investors, vendors, and customers suffered significant financial harm.

LESSONS LEARNED

The Fyre Festival's failure underscores the catastrophic impact of operating without documented and followed systems:

- **Chaos Ensues Without Systems:** Lack of clear procedures led to disorganization and failure to deliver on promises.
- **Customer Trust Erodes:** Inconsistency and unmet expectations destroyed credibility.
- **Legal and Financial Ramifications:** Non-compliance with industry standards and contractual obligations resulted in severe consequences.

The collapse of the Fyre Festival serves as a stark reminder of what can happen when systems are neglected or completely absent. Documented processes, structured project plans, and effective communication are not just formalities—they are the backbone of any successful operation. Without them, even the grandest vision will disintegrate into chaos. The festival's disastrous outcome illustrates how a lack of systems doesn't just damage operations; it can destroy reputations, erode trust, and lead to significant legal and financial repercussions. In the end, it's not enough to have big ideas—you need the systems in place to bring them to life in a reliable, consistent, and executable manner.

CONCLUSION: BUILDING YOUR SOLID FOUNDATION

Systems are the bedrock upon which successful organizations are built. They provide the structure and guidance necessary for consistent performance, employee empowerment, and customer satisfaction.

Key Takeaways:

- **Document Your Processes:** Clear, accessible documentation is essential for consistency and scalability.
- **Engage Your Team:** Involve employees in developing and refining systems to enhance buy-in and effectiveness.
- **Balance System Design and Execution:** Both elements must work in harmony to achieve optimal results.
- **Learn from Real-World Examples:** Emulate successes like McDonald's, and heed the cautionary tales like the Fyre Festival.

Remember, even the most talented team needs well-defined systems to channel their efforts productively. By investing in robust systems, you lay the groundwork for sustainable success and continuous improvement.

As we move to the next chapter, we'll explore how measuring the right things can guide your journey—much like how a compass and map are essential companions on any expedition. So, turn the page, and let's navigate the world of **Measurement** together.

CHAPTER 5:

MEASUREMENT – NAVIGATING WITH DATA

BY KENDALL PETERSON

Imagine driving a car with a blacked-out windshield, relying solely on the soothing voice of your GPS saying, "You're on the fastest route." Sounds terrifying, right? Yet, many businesses operate in a similar fashion—moving forward without clear visibility, hoping for the best. **Measurement** is the windshield that lets you see the road ahead, the dashboard that tells you how fast you're going, and the fuel gauge that warns you before you end up stranded on the side of the road.

In this chapter, we'll explore the critical role of Measurement in steering your organization toward success. We'll delve into how collecting the right data informs decision-making, enables proactive management, and helps avoid costly detours. We'll also examine real-world examples of companies that have mastered the art of Measurement, as well as those that learned the hard way what happens when you fly blind.

So, buckle up, adjust your mirrors, and let's hit the road toward data-driven excellence.

UNDERSTANDING MEASUREMENT

Collecting the Right Facts to Inform Decision-Making
In the age of information, data is the new oil—valuable, powerful, and capable of fueling remarkable growth when refined properly. **Measurement** involves collecting relevant data (facts) about your organization's

performance, processes, and environment to make informed decisions.

Key Aspects:

- **Relevance:** Focus on data that directly impacts your goals and objectives.
- **Accuracy:** Ensure the data is reliable and free from errors.
- **Timeliness:** Collect and analyze data promptly to make swift decisions.

By gathering the right facts, you move from gut-feeling management to evidence-based leadership, reducing uncertainty and enhancing confidence in your choices.

The Analogy of a Car Dashboard for Business Metrics

Think of your business metrics as the gauges on your car's dashboard:

- **Speedometer (Revenue Growth):** Shows how quickly your business is expanding.
- **Fuel Gauge (Cash Flow):** Indicates how much financial fuel you have left before needing a refill.
- **Engine Light (Operational Efficiency):** Warns of internal issues that require attention.
- **GPS (Strategic Direction):** Guides you toward your long-term goals.

Without these indicators, you'd be guessing your speed, running out of fuel unexpectedly, or missing critical maintenance—leading to breakdowns and setbacks.

Similarly, in business, having a dashboard of key metrics allows you to monitor performance, identify trends, and take corrective actions before small issues become major problems.

WHY MEASUREMENT MATTERS

Running the Business by Objective Data Rather Than Intuition

While intuition and experience have their place, relying solely on them is akin to gambling. Measurement brings objectivity to the table:

- **Removes Bias:** Data doesn't have personal preferences or blind spots.
- **Enhances Transparency:** Decisions can be traced back to concrete evidence.
- **Facilitates Accountability:** Performance can be measured against agreed-upon standards.

For example, rather than assuming a marketing campaign is effective because it "feels right," measuring conversion rates, customer acquisition costs, and return on investment provides a factual basis for evaluation.

Enabling Proactive Management and Problem-Solving

Measurement allows you to anticipate challenges and seize opportunities:

- **Early Detection:** Spot negative trends before they escalate.
- **Informed Forecasting:** Predict future performance based on historical data.
- **Resource Optimization:** Allocate resources to areas with the highest potential impact.

By staying ahead of the curve, you can navigate obstacles with agility and capitalize on market shifts more effectively than competitors who react only after the fact.

CREATING A DASHBOARD

Identifying Key Performance Indicators (KPIs)

Key Performance Indicators (KPIs) are measurable values that demonstrate how effectively your organization is achieving its critical objectives. Selecting the right KPIs is essential:

- **Align with Goals:** KPIs should reflect what matters most to your organization's success.
- **Be Measurable:** Quantifiable data allows for objective assessment.
- **Be Actionable:** KPIs should inform decisions and inspire action.

Examples of KPIs:

- **Financial:** Revenue growth rate, profit margins, return on investment.
- **Customer:** Satisfaction scores, retention rates, net promoter score.
- **Operational:** Production efficiency, quality defect rates, supply chain metrics.
- **Employee:** Engagement levels, turnover rates, training effectiveness.

Ensuring Data Accuracy and Relevance

Collecting data is one thing; ensuring it's accurate and relevant is another. Poor-quality data can lead to misguided decisions.

Strategies for Data Integrity:

- **Standardize Data Collection:** Use consistent methods and definitions.
- **Automate Where Possible:** Reduce human error through automation.
- **Validate Regularly:** Cross-check data for discrepancies and correct them promptly.
- **Update KPIs:** Regularly review KPIs to ensure they remain aligned with evolving goals.

By maintaining high data quality, you build trust in the metrics and the decisions derived from them.

PRACTICAL APPLICATION - MEASUREMENT

Implementing Systems for Real-Time Data Collection

Real-time data provides immediate insights, allowing for swift action. Implementing systems to collect data in real time involves:

- **Investing in Technology:** Utilize software and tools that automate data collection and reporting.
- **Integrating Systems:** Ensure different platforms communicate seamlessly (e.g., CRM, ERP, analytics tools).
- **Customizing Dashboards:** Tailor dashboards to display relevant KPIs at a glance.
- **Ensuring Accessibility:** Make data available to those who need it when they need it.

Benefits:

- **Improved Responsiveness:** Quickly address issues as they arise.
- **Enhanced Collaboration:** Share insights across teams to align efforts.
- **Continuous Improvement:** Monitor the impact of changes in real time.

Training Teams to Interpret and Act on Data Insights

Data is only valuable if it leads to action. Training your team to understand and utilize data involves:

- **Educational Programs:** Offer workshops or courses on data literacy and analytics.
- **User-Friendly Tools:** Provide intuitive platforms that simplify data interpretation.
- **Encouraging a Data-Driven Culture:** Promote curiosity and questioning based on data insights.
- **Recognition and Incentives:** Reward teams and individuals who effectively leverage data to achieve results.

Empowering your team with data skills enhances decision-making at all levels and fosters innovation.

POSITIVE USE CASE - MEASUREMENT

A Company's Transformation Through Data-Driven Strategies: Netflix

Background:
In the late 1990s, **Netflix** began as a DVD-by-mail service, competing with brick-and-mortar rental stores like Blockbuster. Recognizing the potential of streaming technology and the power of data, Netflix transformed itself into a leading global entertainment provider.

| LEVERAGING DATA ANALYTICS

Personalized Recommendations:

- **Data Collection:** Netflix tracks viewing habits, search queries, ratings, and even the time of day users watch content.
- **Algorithm Development:** Advanced algorithms analyze this data to predict what users might enjoy.
- **User Experience:** Personalized recommendations keep subscribers engaged, increasing satisfaction and reducing churn.

Content Creation:

- **Data-Driven Production:** Netflix uses viewer data to inform decisions about original content creation.

- **Success Stories:** Shows like *House of Cards* were greenlit based on data indicating a high probability of success due to viewer preferences.

IMPROVED FORECASTING AND RESOURCE ALLOCATION

Strategic Investments:

- **Market Expansion:** Data helps identify regions with growth potential, guiding marketing and infrastructure investments.
- **Budget Optimization:** Analytics inform how much to invest in content, balancing cost with anticipated viewer engagement.

Operational Efficiency:

- **Server Optimization:** Data on streaming patterns enables efficient distribution of resources to minimize buffering and downtime.
- **Customer Support:** Analytics identify common issues, allowing proactive solutions and improved customer service.

Impact

- **Subscriber Growth:** Netflix's subscriber base grew exponentially, reaching over 200 million worldwide.

- **Competitive Advantage:** The company's data-driven approach set it apart from competitors slow to adopt similar strategies.
- **Industry Disruption:** Netflix revolutionized how content is consumed and produced, influencing the entire entertainment industry.

By embracing Measurement and leveraging data analytics, Netflix transformed from a DVD rental service into a global streaming giant. Their data-driven strategies enabled better forecasting, resource allocation, and customer engagement, illustrating the profound impact of effective Measurement.

NEGATIVE USE CASE - MEASUREMENT

The Dangers of Flying Blind Without Proper Metrics: BlackBerry

In the early 2000s, **BlackBerry** (formerly Research In Motion) was a dominant player in the smartphone market. Known for its physical keyboards and secure email capabilities, BlackBerry devices were the go-to choice for professionals and businesses.

FAILURE TO ADAPT TO MARKET CHANGES

Ignoring Consumer Trends:

- **Touchscreen Revolution:** The launch of the iPhone in 2007 signaled a shift toward touchscreen devices. BlackBerry underestimated consumer appetite for touchscreens and apps.
- **Lack of Data-Driven Insight:** BlackBerry relied on its existing success and did not adequately measure changing customer preferences.

Missed Opportunities:

- **App Ecosystem:** While competitors built extensive app stores, BlackBerry lagged, failing to recognize the importance of third-party applications.

- **Consumer Market:** The company focused on enterprise customers, neglecting data indicating the growing consumer smartphone market.

MISSED OPPORTUNITIES AND UNFORESEEN RISKS

Declining Market Share:

- **Competitor Advancement:** Companies like Apple and Samsung capitalized on data-driven insights into consumer behavior, capturing market share.
- **Sales Plummet:** Without adapting to market trends, BlackBerry's sales declined sharply.

Operational Challenges:

- **Inventory Issues:** Overproduction of outdated models led to financial losses.
- **R&D Missteps:** Investments in features consumers didn't value resulted in wasted resources.

Impact

- **Financial Decline:** BlackBerry's stock price and revenues fell dramatically.
- **Loss of Relevance:** The brand became synonymous with missed opportunities and resistance to change.

- **Restructuring:** The company underwent layoffs and shifted focus to software and services in a bid to survive.

BlackBerry's failure to employ effective Measurement led to a disconnect between their offerings and market demands. By not collecting and acting on the right data, they missed critical shifts in consumer preferences and technological advancements. This oversight underscores the dangers of flying blind without proper metrics, resulting in unforeseen risks and a dramatic fall from industry leadership.

CONCLUSION: NAVIGATING WITH CONFIDENCE

Measurement is not just a technical necessity; it's a strategic imperative. It provides the visibility and insights needed to steer your organization through a complex and ever-changing landscape.

Key Takeaways:

- **Collect Relevant Data:** Focus on metrics that align with your goals and inform decision-making.
- **Ensure Data Quality:** Accurate and timely data builds trust and enhances effectiveness.
- **Empower Your Team:** Train and equip your team to interpret data and act on insights.

- **Learn from Others:** Emulate companies like Netflix that harness data for growth, and avoid the pitfalls experienced by BlackBerry.

By embracing Measurement, you transform uncertainty into clarity, risks into opportunities, and data into a powerful ally. Just as a skilled driver relies on their dashboard to navigate safely and efficiently, a successful organization uses Measurement to guide its journey toward sustained success.

As we continue our exploration, the next chapter will delve into the importance of **Relationships**—the connections that fuel collaboration, loyalty, and growth. After all, even with the best data and systems, it's the people and partnerships that bring strategies to life. So, turn the page, and let's build bridges together.

CHAPTER 6:

RELATIONSHIPS – CULTIVATING CONNECTIONS

Imagine trying to play a game of basketball all by yourself—no teammates to pass to, no opponents to challenge you, and no crowd to cheer you on. Sure, you might improve your dribbling skills, but without others, the game loses its purpose and excitement. In the business world, **Relationships** are the dynamic interplay that brings energy, opportunity, and meaning to your endeavors. They are the connections that transform solitary efforts into collaborative successes.

In this chapter, we'll explore the vital role that Relationships play in achieving business excellence. We'll delve into how building trust and mutual respect with clients, vendors, employees, and other stakeholders can propel your organization forward. Through real-world examples, we'll illustrate both the triumphs of strategic relationship management and the pitfalls of neglecting this essential factor.

So, lace up your sneakers, and let's hit the court of connection and collaboration!

DEFINING RELATIONSHIPS

The Role of Relationships with Clients, Vendors, and Employees

At its core, a business is a network of relationships. These connections span various groups:

- **Clients/Customers:** The lifeblood of your organization. Their satisfaction and loyalty drive revenue and growth.
- **Vendors/Suppliers:** Partners who provide the goods and services that enable your operations.
- **Employees:** The internal team that executes your vision and interacts with customers and partners.
- **Community and Stakeholders:** The broader ecosystem, including investors, regulators, and the public.

Each relationship contributes to your organization's success. Understanding and nurturing these connections is not just beneficial—it's imperative.

BUILDING TRUST AND MUTUAL RESPECT

Trust is the currency of relationships. Without it, transactions become burdensome, negotiations stall, and collaborations falter. Mutual respect fosters open communication, alignment, and synergy.

Key Components:

- **Integrity:** Honoring commitments and acting ethically.
- **Transparency:** Communicating openly and honestly.
- **Empathy:** Understanding and valuing others' perspectives.

- **Reliability:** Consistently delivering on promises.

Building trust and respect requires ongoing effort but pays dividends in loyalty, cooperation, and goodwill.

WHY RELATIONSHIPS MATTER

Predictor of Success Based on the Number and Quality of Relationships

In his book *Never Eat Alone*, Keith Ferrazzi emphasizes that success is not just about what you know but who you know—and how well you know them. High-quality relationships can:

- **Open Doors:** Provide access to opportunities, resources, and information.
- **Enhance Reputation:** Positive relationships build credibility and attract others.
- **Facilitate Growth:** Collaborative partnerships can lead to innovation and expansion.

The strength and breadth of your relationships often correlate with your ability to achieve and sustain success.

Impact on Customer Retention and Word-of-Mouth Referrals

Happy customers don't just provide repeat business; they become advocates. Word-of-mouth referrals are among the most powerful marketing tools, fueled by strong relationships.

Benefits:

- **Increased Lifetime Value:** Loyal customers spend more over time.
- **Reduced Acquisition Costs:** Referrals lower the expense of attracting new customers.
- **Competitive Advantage:** Exceptional relationship management differentiates you in the market.

Conversely, poor relationships can lead to churn, negative reviews, and reputational damage.

BUILDING HEALTHY RELATIONSHIPS

Strategies for Establishing Strong Connections

1. **Active Listening:** Pay attention to others' needs, concerns, and feedback.
2. **Personalization:** Tailor interactions to reflect individual preferences and histories.
3. **Consistency:** Maintain regular and meaningful contact.
4. **Value Addition:** Offer support, resources, or insights that benefit others.
5. **Cultural Sensitivity:** Respect and adapt to diverse backgrounds and norms.

Building relationships is not a one-time event but an ongoing process that requires intentionality and sincerity.

MAINTAINING AND NURTURING RELATIONSHIPS OVER TIME

Relationships, like plants, need care to flourish. Nurturing involves:

- **Celebrating Milestones:** Recognize achievements, anniversaries, or special occasions.
- **Providing Support:** Be there during challenges, offering assistance or simply a listening ear.
- **Seeking Feedback:** Encourage open dialogue to strengthen the connection.
- **Adapting to Change:** Stay attuned to evolving needs and adjust accordingly.

By investing time and effort, you cultivate relationships that endure and deepen over time.

PRACTICAL APPLICATION - RELATIONSHIPS

Communication Techniques to Deepen Relationships

- **Empathetic Communication:** Show genuine interest and understanding.
- **Clarity and Transparency:** Be open about intentions, expectations, and limitations.
- **Positive Reinforcement:** Acknowledge and appreciate contributions and qualities.
- **Conflict Resolution Skills:** Address disagreements constructively and promptly.

Effective communication is the bridge that connects hearts and minds, fostering trust and collaboration.

Aligning Organizational Practices with Relationship Goals

- **Customer-Centric Policies:** Design procedures that prioritize customer satisfaction.
- **Employee Engagement Programs:** Create a workplace culture that values and supports staff.
- **Vendor Partnerships:** Develop mutually beneficial agreements and open lines of communication.
- **Community Involvement:** Engage in corporate social responsibility initiatives that reflect shared values.

Aligning practices with relationship goals ensures that actions consistently reinforce the importance of connections.

POSITIVE USE CASE - RELATIONSHIPS

Success Achieved Through Strategic Partnerships: Starbucks and Howard Schultz's Vision

Background:

In the 1980s, **Starbucks** was a small chain of coffee shops in Seattle. Howard Schultz joined the company and later acquired it, envisioning not just a place to grab coffee but a "third place" between home and work where people could relax, connect, and experience community.

BUILDING RELATIONSHIPS WITH CUSTOMERS

Creating the Starbucks Experience:

- **Personalized Service:** Baristas learn customers' names and preferences.
- **Welcoming Environment:** Stores are designed for comfort and social interaction.
- **Customer Engagement:** Feedback is encouraged, and loyalty programs reward patronage.

Impact:

- **Customer Loyalty:** High levels of repeat business and brand advocacy.

- **Global Community:** Starbucks stores become hubs of social interaction worldwide.

CULTIVATING EMPLOYEE RELATIONSHIPS

Investing in Partners:

- **Employee Benefits:** Offers healthcare, stock options, and college tuition assistance even to part-time employees.
- **Inclusive Culture:** Refers to employees as "partners," fostering a sense of ownership.
- **Training and Development:** Emphasizes personal and professional growth.

Impact:

- **Employee Satisfaction:** Lower turnover rates compared to industry averages.
- **Enhanced Service:** Engaged employees provide better customer experiences.

STRATEGIC VENDOR PARTNERSHIPS

Ethical Sourcing:

- **Fair Trade Practices:** Builds relationships with coffee farmers, ensuring fair prices.

- **Sustainability Initiatives:** Collaborates on environmental practices and community development.

Impact:

- **Quality Products:** Access to high-quality coffee beans.
- **Brand Reputation:** Recognized as a socially responsible company.

By strategically cultivating relationships with customers, employees, and suppliers, Starbucks transformed from a local coffee shop into a global phenomenon. The company's success illustrates how deep connections and mutual respect can drive loyalty, growth, and a lasting legacy.

NEGATIVE USE CASE - RELATIONSHIPS

Business Decline Due to Neglected Relationships: Uber's Reputation Challenges

Background:
Founded in 2009, **Uber** revolutionized the transportation industry with its ride-sharing app. Rapid growth catapulted the company into markets worldwide. However, a series of relationship missteps led to significant challenges.

POOR RELATIONSHIPS WITH DRIVERS

Issues:

- **Classification Controversies:** Treating drivers as independent contractors without benefits.
- **Lack of Support:** Drivers felt undervalued and unsupported by the company.
- **Fare Cuts:** Reductions in fares without adequate driver input or compensation adjustments.

Impact:

- **Driver Dissatisfaction:** Protests, strikes, and high turnover rates.
- **Legal Battles:** Lawsuits over employment status and rights.

CUSTOMER TRUST EROSION

Issues:

- **Safety Concerns:** Reports of passenger harassment and assault.
- **Surge Pricing Controversies:** Perceived price gouging during peak times or emergencies.
- **Privacy Violations:** Mishandling of customer data and "God View" tool misuse.

Impact:

- **Public Backlash:** Negative media coverage and social media campaigns like #DeleteUber.
- **Loss of Market Share:** Customers switched to competitors like Lyft.

INTERNAL CULTURE PROBLEMS

Issues:

- **Toxic Work Environment:** Allegations of harassment, discrimination, and unethical behavior.
- **Leadership Scandals:** CEO Travis Kalanick's confrontations and controversial comments.

Impact:

- **Employee Disengagement:** Low morale and departures of key talent.
- **Reputational Damage:** Difficulty attracting and retaining top employees.

REPUTATION DAMAGE FROM POOR STAKEHOLDER INTERACTIONS

Overall Consequences:

- **Financial Losses:** Decreased valuations and investor concerns.
- **Regulatory Scrutiny:** Bans and restrictions in several cities and countries.
- **Leadership Overhaul:** Forced resignation of the CEO and significant board changes.

Uber's neglect of relationships with drivers, customers, employees, and regulators led to substantial setbacks. The company's experience underscores the critical importance of cultivating and maintaining healthy relationships. Neglecting this factor can result in trust erosion, legal challenges, financial losses, and lasting reputational harm.

CONCLUSION: BUILDING BRIDGES TO SUCCESS

Relationships are not just a "soft" aspect of business; they are a strategic asset that can drive success or precipitate failure. By investing in connections built on trust and mutual respect, you lay the groundwork for sustainable growth and a positive impact.

Key Takeaways:

- **Prioritize Trust:** Act with integrity and transparency to build strong foundations.
- **Engage Actively:** Listen, communicate, and adapt to the needs of your stakeholders.
- **Align Practices with Values:** Ensure that organizational policies reinforce the importance of relationships.
- **Learn from Examples:** Emulate companies like Starbucks that excel in relationship management, and heed the warnings from cases like Uber.

Remember, no business operates in a vacuum. The relationships you cultivate become the channels through which opportunities flow, challenges are overcome, and legacies are built.

As we proceed to the next chapter, we'll explore the role of **Communication**—the essential tool that enables relationships to flourish and organizations to thrive. Effective communication is the glue that holds everything together, so turn the page, and let's delve into the art of connecting through words and actions.

CHAPTER 7:

COMMUNICATION – THE GLUE OF THE ORGANIZATION

BY KENDALL PETERSON

Imagine trying to coordinate a symphony without a conductor. Each musician plays their part, but without guidance and synchronization, the result is a cacophony rather than a harmonious masterpiece. In the business world, **Communication** is the conductor's baton—it brings direction, unity, and rhythm to an organization's operations. Without effective communication, even the most talented teams and robust strategies can falter.

In this chapter, we'll explore the pivotal role of Communication as the glue that holds an organization together. We'll delve into how clear and effective communication fosters unity, alleviates anxieties, and drives success. Through real-world examples, we'll illustrate both the triumphs achieved through transparent communication and the pitfalls that arise when communication breaks down.

So, take your place in the orchestra pit, and let's orchestrate a symphony of effective communication!

| UNDERSTANDING COMMUNICATION

The Necessity of Clear and Effective Communication

Communication is more than just the exchange of information; it's the transmission of meaning, intent, and emotion. Effective communication ensures that everyone understands their roles, responsibilities, and how they contribute to the organization's goals.

Key Aspects:

- **Clarity:** Messages should be clear and unambiguous.
- **Consistency:** Information should be consistent across different channels and over time.
- **Timeliness:** Sharing information promptly prevents misinformation and speculation.
- **Appropriateness:** Tailoring the message to the audience's needs and context.

Without clear communication, misunderstandings can occur, leading to errors, wasted resources, and frustration.

INTERNAL AND EXTERNAL COMMUNICATION DYNAMICS

Internal Communication:

- **Vertical Communication:** Between management and employees, encompassing directives, feedback, and reporting.
- **Horizontal Communication:** Among peers and departments, facilitating collaboration and coordination.
- **Informal Communication:** The grapevine, which can influence morale and culture.

External Communication:

- **Customer Interaction:** Marketing, sales, and customer service communications shape brand perception.
- **Stakeholder Engagement:** Communicating with investors, regulators, and partners.
- **Public Relations:** Managing the organization's image and responding to public inquiries.

Balancing internal and external communication ensures that the organization's message is coherent and reinforces its values and objectives.

WHY COMMUNICATION MATTERS

Provides Unity and Direction, Especially During Change
Change is a constant in business, whether it's a new strategy, organizational restructuring, or market shifts. Effective communication during these times is crucial:

- **Sets Expectations:** Clarifies what is changing, why, and how it will affect stakeholders.
- **Reduces Uncertainty:** Alleviates fears and rumors by providing accurate information.
- **Builds Trust:** Demonstrates transparency and respect for those involved.

By keeping everyone informed and engaged, communication unites the organization toward common goals.

Relieves Anxieties and Fosters Inclusion

People naturally seek information to understand their environment. Lack of communication can lead to:

- **Speculation:** Filling the void with assumptions or misinformation.
- **Anxiety:** Worrying about unknowns or potential negative impacts.
- **Disengagement:** Feeling excluded or undervalued.

Effective communication addresses these issues by:

- **Providing Reassurance:** Sharing plans and addressing concerns openly.
- **Encouraging Participation:** Inviting input and feedback to foster a sense of belonging.
- **Acknowledging Contributions:** Recognizing efforts and achievements.

Communication is the bridge that connects leadership with the broader team, fostering a collaborative and supportive culture.

EFFECTIVE COMMUNICATION STRATEGIES

Articulating the Organization's Mission and Progress

Regularly communicating the organization's mission, vision, and progress ensures that everyone understands the bigger picture.

- **Mission Statements:** Clearly define the organization's purpose and values.
- **Progress Updates:** Share achievements, milestones, and challenges.
- **Storytelling:** Use narratives to illustrate the impact of the organization's work.

This approach aligns efforts, motivates employees, and reinforces commitment to shared goals.

Encouraging Open Dialogue and Feedback

Communication is a two-way street. Encouraging dialogue enhances understanding and innovation.

- **Open-Door Policies:** Leaders make themselves accessible for conversations.
- **Feedback Mechanisms:** Surveys, suggestion boxes, and meetings to gather input.
- **Active Listening:** Demonstrate genuine interest in others' perspectives.

By valuing employees' voices, organizations can tap into valuable insights and foster a culture of continuous improvement.

PRACTICAL APPLICATION - COMMUNICATION

Implementing Communication Channels and Protocols
Effective communication requires the right channels and clear protocols.

- **Multi-Channel Approach:** Utilize emails, meetings, intranets, instant messaging, and social media.
- **Define Protocols:** Establish guidelines for frequency, tone, and content of communications.
- **Technology Integration:** Leverage tools like collaboration platforms (e.g., Slack, Microsoft Teams) to streamline communication.

Consistency in channels and protocols ensures that messages are delivered and received as intended.

TAILORING MESSAGES FOR DIFFERENT AUDIENCES

Different stakeholders have varying needs and preferences.

- **Audience Analysis:** Understand the interests, concerns, and language of each group.
- **Customized Content:** Adapt messages to be relevant and engaging for each audience.
- **Cultural Sensitivity:** Respect cultural differences in global organizations.

Tailoring messages enhances comprehension and fosters stronger connections with diverse audiences.

POSITIVE USE CASE - COMMUNICATION

Enhanced Employee Engagement Through Transparent Communication: Microsoft's Cultural Transformation

Background:
In 2014, **Satya Nadella** became the CEO of **Microsoft**, inheriting a company facing internal silos, stiff competition, and a perception of stagnation. Recognizing that effective communication was essential to revitalizing the organization, Nadella embarked on a mission to transform Microsoft's culture.

ARTICULATING A CLEAR VISION

One Microsoft:

- **Unified Mission:** Nadella communicated a refreshed mission: "To empower every person and every organization on the planet to achieve more."
- **Transparent Leadership:** He shared his vision openly through emails, company meetings, and one-on-one interactions.

Impact:

- **Alignment:** Employees understood the new direction and their role in it.

- **Motivation:** The clear and inspiring mission reignited passion within the workforce.

ENCOURAGING OPEN DIALOGUE AND COLLABORATION

Cultural Shift:

- **Growth Mindset:** Nadella promoted a culture of learning and innovation, encouraging employees to take risks and learn from failures.
- **Accessible Leadership:** He maintained an open-door policy and regularly engaged with employees at all levels.
- **Feedback Platforms:** Implemented tools and forums for employees to share ideas and feedback.

Impact:

- **Employee Engagement:** Surveys showed increased job satisfaction and commitment.
- **Innovation Surge:** Collaboration led to breakthroughs like the development of Microsoft Teams and advancements in cloud computing with Azure.

STRENGTHENED BRAND IMAGE VIA CONSISTENT MESSAGING

External Communication:

- **Unified Branding:** Consistent messaging across products and services reinforced Microsoft's new identity.
- **Customer-Centric Approach:** Communication focused on how Microsoft solutions empower users.

Impact:

- **Market Perception:** Microsoft's image shifted from a legacy software provider to a forward-thinking tech leader.
- **Financial Success:** The company's stock price and revenues reached new heights, reflecting renewed investor confidence.

By prioritizing transparent and effective communication, Microsoft under Nadella's leadership revitalized its culture, enhanced employee engagement, and strengthened its brand. This transformation illustrates how communication can be the catalyst for unity, innovation, and sustained success.

NEGATIVE USE CASE - COMMUNICATION

MISUNDERSTANDINGS LEADING TO PROJECT FAILURES: NASA'S CHALLENGER DISASTER

Background:
On January 28, 1986, the **Space Shuttle Challenger** broke apart 73 seconds into its flight, leading to the tragic loss of all seven crew members. An investigation revealed that communication failures within **NASA** and its contractor **Morton Thiokol** were significant contributing factors.

COMMUNICATION BREAKDOWN

Ignored Warnings:

- **Engineer's Concerns:** Engineers at Morton Thiokol raised concerns about the O-ring seals' performance in cold temperatures forecasted for the launch day.
- **Inadequate Transmission:** These concerns were not effectively communicated to higher management levels or were downplayed.

Pressure and Misalignment:

- **Launch Schedule Pressure:** There was immense pressure to maintain the launch schedule due to political and media attention.

- **Cultural Barriers:** A hierarchical culture discouraged open communication and the elevation of dissenting opinions.

EROSION OF TRUST DUE TO MISINFORMATION

Decision-Making Flaws:

- **Lack of Transparency:** Critical information was withheld or not adequately considered in the decision to proceed with the launch.
- **Overconfidence:** Previous successes led to complacency and an underestimation of risks.

Impact:

- **Tragic Loss:** The disaster resulted in the death of the crew, including teacher Christa McAuliffe.
- **Public Trust Erosion:** Confidence in NASA's safety and reliability was severely damaged.
- **Program Suspension:** The shuttle program was halted for nearly three years during the investigation and restructuring.

LESSONS LEARNED

Improving Communication Practices:

- **Organizational Changes:** NASA restructured to promote better communication channels and accountability.
- **Emphasis on Safety:** Established a culture where safety concerns could be raised without fear of retribution.
- **Enhanced Training:** Implemented programs to improve communication skills and decision-making processes.

The Challenger disaster underscores the devastating consequences that can result from communication failures. Misunderstandings, suppressed information, and a lack of open dialogue led to a preventable tragedy. This case highlights the critical need for transparent and effective communication, especially in high-stakes environments.

CONCLUSION: HARMONIZING THE ORGANIZATION THROUGH COMMUNICATION

Communication is the lifeblood of any organization. It connects people, aligns efforts, and propels the organization toward its goals. Whether navigating change, fostering innovation, or building relationships, effective communication is the tool that makes it possible.

Key Takeaways:

- **Promote Transparency:** Open and honest communication builds trust and engagement.
- **Encourage Dialogue:** Two-way communication empowers employees and taps into collective wisdom.
- **Tailor Your Message:** Adapting communication to different audiences enhances understanding and connection.
- **Learn from Examples:** Emulate successful communication strategies like those implemented by Microsoft, and recognize the risks highlighted by events like the Challenger disaster.

Remember, communication is not just about transmitting information; it's about connecting people and ideas. By mastering the art of communication, you strengthen the glue that holds your organization together, enabling it to perform like a well-conducted symphony.

As we move forward, the next chapter will explore **Innovation**—the driving force that keeps organizations ahead of the curve. Communication lays the foundation, and innovation builds upon it to create the future. So, turn the page, and let's embark on a journey of creativity and progress.

CHAPTER 8:

INNOVATION – STAYING AHEAD OF THE CURVE

BY KENDALL PETERSON

Imagine you're at a dance party, and everyone suddenly starts doing the latest viral dance move, but you're still doing the Macarena. Awkward, right? In the business world, **Innovation** is that new dance move—it keeps you in sync with the times and prevents you from becoming the person everyone whispers about. Innovation isn't just about flashy new products; it's about solving problems, staying relevant, and continuously adapting in a changing market.

In this chapter, we'll explore the critical role of Innovation in preventing stagnation and driving competitiveness. We'll delve into how embracing change and refreshing old ideas can propel your organization forward. Through real-world examples, we'll illustrate both the triumphs achieved through innovative thinking and the downfalls of companies that failed to adapt.

So, put on your creative hat, and let's groove to the rhythm of Innovation!

DEFINING INNOVATION

Solving Problems and Staying Relevant in a Changing Market

At its core, **Innovation** is about creating value through new ideas, processes, products, or services. It's not just about invention but about implementing changes that meet evolving customer needs and market demands.

Key Aspects:

- **Problem-Solving:** Addressing existing challenges or inefficiencies.
- **Value Creation:** Enhancing customer experiences or creating new markets.
- **Adaptability:** Responding to technological advances and societal shifts.

Innovation keeps your organization relevant by ensuring that you're not just reacting to changes but proactively shaping the future.

THE DANGERS OF COMPLACENCY

Complacency is the silent killer of progress. When organizations rest on their laurels, they risk:

- **Obsolescence:** Products or services become outdated.
- **Loss of Market Share:** Competitors seize opportunities you've overlooked.
- **Decline in Customer Loyalty:** Customers migrate to more innovative alternatives.

Remember, even if you're on the right track, you'll get run over if you just sit there.

| WHY INNOVATION MATTERS

Prevents Stagnation and Decline

Without innovation, organizations become stagnant, like a pond collecting algae. Innovation breathes fresh air into your business:

- **Stimulates Growth:** Opens new revenue streams and markets.
- **Enhances Efficiency:** Improves processes and reduces costs.
- **Invigorates Culture:** Encourages creativity and engagement among employees.

Innovation keeps the momentum going, ensuring that your organization doesn't become yesterday's news.

Drives Continuous Improvement and Competitiveness

In a world where change is the only constant, innovation is your competitive edge:

- **Differentiation:** Sets you apart from competitors.
- **Customer Satisfaction:** Meets and exceeds evolving expectations.
- **Market Leadership:** Positions you as an industry pioneer.

By continuously innovating, you stay ahead of the curve, leading rather than following.

EMBRACING CHANGE

Proactively Adapting to Market Shifts

Successful organizations anticipate changes and adapt proactively:

- **Market Research:** Stay informed about trends, customer behaviors, and emerging technologies.
- **Agility:** Be prepared to pivot strategies in response to new information.
- **Risk-Taking:** Embrace calculated risks to explore new opportunities.

Proactive adaptation means you're the one setting the pace, not scrambling to catch up.

Refreshing Old Ideas and Methods

Innovation isn't always about creating something entirely new; sometimes, it's about reimagining existing concepts:

- **Process Improvements:** Streamline operations for better efficiency.
- **Product Enhancements:** Update offerings to add value.
- **Business Model Innovation:** Alter how you deliver value to customers.

By refreshing old ideas, you can breathe new life into your organization without reinventing the wheel.

PRACTICAL APPLICATION - INNOVATION

Fostering a Culture of Creativity and Experimentation

An innovative organization cultivates an environment where new ideas flourish:

- **Encourage Curiosity:** Promote questioning and exploration.
- **Support Experimentation:** Allow room for trial and error without fear of failure.
- **Cross-Functional Collaboration:** Bring together diverse perspectives to spark creativity.

Creating a culture of innovation empowers employees to contribute ideas that drive the organization forward.

Investing in Research and Development

Innovation often requires investment:

- **Allocate Resources:** Dedicate budget and time to R&D initiatives.
- **Partner with External Experts:** Collaborate with universities, startups, or research institutions.
- **Leverage Technology:** Utilize cutting-edge tools and platforms to enhance innovation efforts.

Investing in innovation is an investment in your organization's future.

POSITIVE USE CASE - INNOVATION

A Company's Resurgence Through Innovative Products/Services: Apple Inc.

Background:

In the late 1990s, **Apple Inc.** was on the brink of bankruptcy. Struggling with declining market share and uninspiring product lines, the company needed a radical change. The return of co-founder Steve Jobs marked the beginning of a remarkable turnaround driven by innovation.

> **GAINING MARKET SHARE BY ANTICIPATING, AND GENERATING, CUSTOMER NEED**

Innovative Products:

- **iMac (1998):** A bold, colorful, all-in-one computer that simplified user experience and reignited interest in Apple's products.
- **iPod (2001):** Revolutionized the music industry by allowing users to carry thousands of songs in their pocket.
- **iPhone (2007):** Transformed the smartphone market with its touchscreen interface and integration of phone, internet, and iPod functionalities.
- **iPad (2010):** Created a new category of devices between smartphones and laptops.

Strategies:

- **User-Centric Design:** Focused on intuitive interfaces and sleek aesthetics.
- **Ecosystem Development:** Created a seamless experience across devices with services like iTunes and the App Store.
- **Marketing Genius:** Leveraged impactful advertising to communicate the value of their innovations.

Impact:

- **Market Leadership:** Apple became one of the world's most valuable companies.
- **Industry Disruption:** Set new standards in multiple industries, forcing competitors to adapt.
- **Customer Loyalty:** Cultivated a dedicated customer base eager for each new release.

By relentlessly pursuing innovation and anticipating customer needs, Apple transformed from a struggling company into a global powerhouse. Their commitment to innovation not only revitalized their brand but also reshaped entire industries.

NEGATIVE USE CASE - INNOVATION

The Downfall of Industry Giants Who Failed to Innovate: Blockbuster LLC

Background:
In the 1990s, **Blockbuster** was the leading video rental company, with thousands of stores worldwide. They dominated the market, and a Friday night visit to Blockbuster was a routine for many families. However, technological advances and changing consumer behaviors signaled a shift in the industry.

LOSS OF RELEVANCE AND MARKET POSITION

Missed Opportunities:

- **Dismissed Netflix's Proposal:** In 2000, Netflix approached Blockbuster with a proposal to handle Blockbuster's online brand while Blockbuster would promote Netflix in its stores. Blockbuster declined, viewing Netflix's model as a niche market.
- **Ignored Shift to Streaming:** Blockbuster continued focusing on physical rentals, underestimating the growing demand for online streaming services.
- **Late Adoption:** By the time Blockbuster introduced its own DVD-by-mail and streaming services, competitors had already captured the market.

Complacency Elements:

- **Overconfidence in Brand:** Believed their established brand and customer base would sustain them.
- **Underestimating Consumer Preferences:** Failed to recognize the inconvenience of late fees and the appeal of on-demand content.
- **Resistance to Change:** Reluctance to shift from a profitable existing model to an unproven one.

Impact:

- **Financial Decline:** Revenues plummeted as customers migrated to Netflix and other streaming platforms.
- **Bankruptcy:** In 2010, Blockbuster filed for bankruptcy protection.
- **Store Closures:** Nearly all Blockbuster stores were closed, leaving only one remaining franchise store in Bend, Oregon.

Blockbuster's failure to innovate and adapt to changing market conditions led to its downfall. By ignoring technological advancements and evolving customer needs, they lost their market position and became a cautionary tale of complacency.

CONCLUSION: EMBRACING THE DANCE OF INNOVATION

Innovation is not a luxury; it's a necessity for survival and growth in today's fast-paced world. It requires a willingness to challenge the status quo, take risks, and embrace change.

Key Takeaways:

- **Stay Curious:** Continuously explore new ideas and possibilities.
- **Be Proactive:** Anticipate market shifts and adapt before being forced to react.
- **Cultivate a Culture of Innovation:** Empower your team to experiment and contribute creatively.
- **Invest in the Future:** Allocate resources to research and development initiatives.

By learning from Apple's success in leveraging innovation to transform and lead, and from Blockbuster's failure to adapt and subsequent decline, you can position your organization to stay ahead of the curve.

Remember, innovation is like a dance—it's dynamic, requires practice, and is more enjoyable when everyone joins in. So, put on your dancing shoes, encourage your team to groove, and keep moving forward with creativity and adaptability.

As we approach the final chapters, we'll explore how all the elements we've discussed come together to create a cohesive and successful organization. Innovation may be the spark, but it's the synergy of Purpose, Team, Systems, Measurement, Relationships, Communication, and Innovation that truly drives excellence. Turn the page, and let's bring it all together.

CHAPTER 9:

BRINGING THE 7 ELEMENTS TOGETHER

BY KENDALL PETERSON

Imagine you're attempting to bake the world's most delicious cake. You've gathered the finest ingredients—each exceptional on its own—but the magic happens when you combine them in just the right way. Similarly, in business, each of the seven elements we've explored is powerful individually, but their true potential is unleashed when they work together in harmony.

In this chapter, we'll revisit the key insights from each factor, explore how they synergize to create a compounded effect, and discuss strategies for overcoming common challenges in integrating them. So, preheat your organizational oven, and let's blend these ingredients into a recipe for success!

RECAP OF THE ESSENTIAL ELEMENTS

Summarizing Key Insights from Each Factor

1. **Purpose – Charting the Course**
   - **Key Insight:** A clear and compelling Purpose provides direction, motivates stakeholders, and aligns efforts toward a common goal.
   - **Real-World Example:** NASA's Apollo Program succeeded by uniting around President Kennedy's vision to land a man on the Moon, demonstrating the power of a well-defined Purpose.

2. **Team – The Right People in the Right Roles**
   - **Key Insight:** Building a Team of individuals who align with your core values and are placed in roles that leverage their strengths leads to enhanced performance and cohesion.
   - **Real-World Example:** Southwest Airlines prioritized cultural fit and strategic hiring, resulting in exceptional customer service and financial success.

3. **Systems – Building a Foundation for Consistency**
   - **Key Insight:** Documented and well-executed Systems ensure consistency, efficiency, and scalability, providing a solid foundation for operations.
   - **Real-World Example:** McDonald's standardized processes allowed them to deliver consistent quality globally, empowering employees and satisfying customers.

4. **Measurement – Navigating with Data**
   - **Key Insight:** Utilizing accurate and relevant data through Measurement enables informed decision-making, proactive management, and continuous improvement.
   - **Real-World Example:** Netflix leveraged data analytics to personalize user experiences and guide content creation, transforming them into an entertainment giant.

5. **Relationships – Cultivating Connections**
   - **Key Insight:** Building strong Relationships with clients, vendors, employees, and stakeholders fosters trust, loyalty, and collaboration, driving success.
   - **Real-World Example:** Starbucks cultivated deep connections with customers and employees, creating a loyal community and a thriving global brand.

6. **Communication – The Glue of the Organization**
   - **Key Insight:** Clear and effective Communication unites the organization, fosters inclusion, and ensures alignment with goals and values.
   - **Real-World Example:** Microsoft's cultural transformation under Satya Nadella emphasized transparent communication, enhancing employee engagement and innovation.

7. **Innovation – Staying Ahead of the Curve**
   - **Key Insight:** Embracing Innovation prevents stagnation, drives competitiveness, and keeps the organization relevant in a changing market.
   - **Real-World Example:** Apple's relentless pursuit of innovation transformed them from near bankruptcy to a market leader, reshaping entire industries.

REINFORCING THE IMPORTANCE OF INTEGRATING ALL ELEMENTS

Each factor contributes a vital element to the organization's success:

- **Purpose** sets the destination.
- **Team** provides the crew.
- **Systems** offer the map and compass.
- **Measurement** supplies the navigation tools.
- **Relationships** build alliances.
- **Communication** ensures everyone stays connected.
- **Innovation** keeps the journey dynamic and adaptive.

Individually, they address specific areas, but together, they create a comprehensive framework that propels the organization toward its goals. Ignoring any factor is like sailing with a hole in your ship—it hampers progress and may ultimately lead to failure.

THE SYNERGY OF THE ELEMENTS

How the Elements Complement and Enhance Each Other

Consider how these Elements interplay:

- **Purpose and Team:**
  - A clear Purpose attracts and motivates the right Team.
  - The Team brings the Purpose to life through their skills and alignment with values.

- **Systems and Measurement:**
  - Systems establish consistent processes, while Measurement evaluates their effectiveness.
  - Together, they enable continuous improvement and operational excellence.

- **Relationships and Communication:**
  - Strong Relationships are built through effective Communication.
  - Communication fosters trust and collaboration, enhancing Relationships.

- **Innovation and All Elements:**
  - Innovation thrives in an environment where Purpose inspires, the Team is engaged, Systems support creativity, Measurement guides progress, Relationships provide insights, and Communication shares ideas.

THE COMPOUNDED BENEFITS OF HOLISTIC IMPLEMENTATION

When these elements are integrated:

- **Enhanced Efficiency:** Systems and Measurement streamline operations, reducing waste and increasing productivity.
- **Improved Adaptability:** Innovation, supported by a strong Team and clear Purpose, enables swift responses to market changes.
- **Increased Loyalty:** Relationships and Communication build customer and employee loyalty, reducing turnover and fostering advocacy.
- **Sustainable Growth:** The synergy creates a resilient organization capable of sustained success and competitiveness.

Think of it as a well-conducted orchestra. Each instrument (factor) contributes to the symphony, but it's their synchronization that creates beautiful music.

REAL-WORLD EXAMPLE OF SYNERGY: AMAZON

Amazon exemplifies the power of integrating these elements:

- **Purpose:** To be Earth's most customer-centric company.

- **Team:** Hires individuals who are innovative and customer-obsessed.
- **Systems:** Implements efficient logistics and technology systems.
- **Measurement:** Uses data to inform every aspect of the business.
- **Relationships:** Cultivates strong partnerships with vendors and focuses on customer relationships.
- **Communication:** Maintains clear internal and external communication channels.
- **Innovation:** Continuously innovates with services like Amazon Web Services (AWS), Kindle, and Alexa.

This holistic approach has propelled Amazon to become one of the most valuable companies globally.

| OVERCOMING CHALLENGES

Addressing Common Obstacles in Adopting the Elements

Implementing The Essential Elements isn't without challenges. Common obstacles include:

1. **Resistance to Change:**
    - **Issue:** Employees may be comfortable with the status quo.

- **Strategy:** Communicate the benefits clearly, involve employees in the process, and provide support during transitions.

2. **Lack of Alignment:**
   - **Issue:** Misalignment between leadership and staff on goals and values.
   - **Strategy:** Reinforce Purpose and values through regular communication and lead by example.

3. **Resource Constraints:**
   - **Issue:** Limited time, budget, or personnel to implement changes.
   - **Strategy:** Prioritize initiatives based on impact, seek efficiencies, and consider phased implementation.

4. **Cultural Barriers:**
   - **Issue:** Existing culture may not support openness, innovation, or collaboration.
   - **Strategy:** Foster a culture shift by modeling desired behaviors, recognizing and rewarding alignment, and addressing negative influences.

5. **Siloed Departments:**
   - **Issue:** Lack of cross-functional collaboration hampers integration.

- **Strategy:** Encourage interdepartmental projects, implement collaboration tools, and break down hierarchical barriers.

STRATEGIES FOR FOSTERING ORGANIZATIONAL BUY-IN

1. **Engage Leadership:**
   - Leaders must champion the initiative, demonstrating commitment and setting the tone.

2. **Communicate Transparently:**
   - Share the vision, goals, and benefits openly.
   - Address concerns and solicit feedback.

3. **Involve Employees:**
   - Include team members in planning and implementation.
   - Empower them to contribute ideas and take ownership.

4. **Provide Training and Support:**
   - Offer resources to develop necessary skills.
   - Support teams through transitions with coaching and mentoring.

5. **Celebrate Successes:**
   o Recognize and reward progress and achievements.
   o Share success stories to motivate and inspire others.

6. **Monitor and Adjust:**
   o Use Measurement to track progress.
   o Be willing to adapt strategies based on feedback and results.

REAL-WORLD EXAMPLE: ADOBE'S SHIFT TO A SUBSCRIPTION MODEL

Challenge:
Adobe transitioned from selling packaged software to a cloud-based subscription model (Creative Cloud). This required integrating multiple elements and overcoming internal and external resistance.

Strategies Implemented:

- **Purpose:** Clarified the vision to provide continuous value to customers.
- **Communication:** Transparently communicated the reasons and benefits to employees and customers.
- **Team Engagement:** Involved employees in developing the new model, fostering buy-in.

- **Systems and Measurement:** Updated systems to support the subscription model and measured customer satisfaction and retention.
- **Innovation:** Leveraged the shift to introduce new features and services.
- **Relationships:** Worked closely with customers to address concerns and enhance value.

The successful transition led to increased recurring revenue, stronger customer relationships, and reinforced Adobe's position as a leader in creative software.

CONCLUSION: THE SYMPHONY OF SUCCESS

Bringing the 7 Elements together creates a powerful, interconnected framework that enhances every aspect of your organization. By understanding and leveraging the synergy among Purpose, Team, Systems, Measurement, Relationships, Communication, and Innovation, you set the stage for sustainable success.

Final Reflections:

- **Holistic Approach:** Recognize that each factor is essential and interconnected.
- **Continuous Effort:** Integration requires ongoing attention and adaptation.

- **Collective Responsibility:** Everyone in the organization plays a role in embracing and embodying these elements.

By overcoming challenges and fostering organizational buy-in, you can transform your organization into a dynamic, resilient, and thriving entity.

So, gather your team, revisit your Purpose, refine your Systems, embrace Measurement, nurture Relationships, communicate effectively, and innovate boldly. The orchestra is assembled, the instruments are tuned, and the audience awaits. It's time to conduct your symphony of success!

CHAPTER 10:

CALL TO ACTION

BY KENDALL PETERSON

Congratulations! You've navigated through the seven transformative elements that can elevate any organization from mediocrity to excellence. Along the way, you've gained insights into what makes the most successful companies tick and what pitfalls to avoid. But here's the thing: simply knowing these principles is not enough. Knowledge, no matter how profound, is utterly powerless without action. It's like having a sports car sitting in your driveway—sleek, powerful, and full of potential, but utterly useless unless you're willing to put the key in the ignition and drive.

This chapter is your ignition key, providing practical steps to put The Essential Elements into motion. Whether you're a seasoned business leader, an aspiring entrepreneur with a vision, or an individual contributor wanting to make a difference, there's a specific path forward for you. These strategies are tailored to your unique role and circumstances, offering you concrete ways to bring each of the seven elements to life within your organization. The goal is to move from theory to practice, from concepts to concrete results, and from good intentions to tangible achievements.

Remember, none of this matters if it stays on the page. Success doesn't happen by absorbing information or by highlighting sections in a book—it happens through the choices you make and the actions you take every single day. No business was ever transformed by a great idea alone. Execution is where dreams are made or broken. So as you read through these calls to action, challenge yourself to identify at least one step you can take immediately to start making a difference in your organization.

So, roll up your sleeves, grab your favorite motivational beverage (whether it's a cup of coffee, a soothing tea, an energy drink, or that mysterious green smoothie your health-conscious friend swears by), and let's turn these insights into action. Because at the end of the day, it's not about what you know—it's about what you do with it. Let's get moving!

FOR BUSINESS LEADERS

Steps to Champion The Essential Elements Within Your Organization

As a business leader, the success of your organization hinges on your ability to translate vision into reality. You set the tone, drive the culture, and ultimately determine the direction of the entire enterprise. That's a lot of weight to carry, but it's also where real transformation begins. The good news is, you're in the perfect position to make these 7 Essential Elements come alive. It's not just about implementing policies or tweaking processes—it's about creating an environment where the Purpose is understood, the Team is empowered, Systems are solid, Measurements are meaningful, Relationships are valued, Communication is clear, and Innovation is celebrated.

But leading this charge takes more than making executive decisions from behind a desk. It requires you to be visible, engaged, and willing to champion these principles yourself. Your actions send ripples through the entire organization, and when you lead by example, you show your team what these elements look like in practice. So, this section is dedicated to giving you concrete steps and strategies that will help you put the theory into action—showing you how to embed these elements into the DNA of your company, starting from the top down.

If you want your organization to thrive, grow, and leave a legacy, it's time to roll up your sleeves and become the living embodiment of The Essential Elements. Here's where it all starts: with you.

Self-Assessment and Reflection
Before jumping into strategic initiatives, take an honest look at how your organization aligns with each of the seven elements, celebrating strengths and acknowledging gaps. Then, seek diverse perspectives from your team and stakeholders to get a full, objective view and build a shared understanding of where improvement is needed.

Then you have a solid base to do the following:

1. **Define or Refine Your Purpose**
    - **Clarify Mission and Vision:** Ensure your organization's Purpose is clear, compelling, and relevant.

- **Communicate Widely:** Share this Purpose through multiple channels—town halls, newsletters, smoke signals (well, maybe not that last one).

2. **Build and Empower Your Team**
   - **Align Roles and Strengths:** Reevaluate whether team members are in the right seats and align roles with individual strengths.
   - **Foster Development:** Invest in training and mentorship programs to enhance skills and engagement.

3. **Establish Robust Systems**
   - **Document Processes:** Ensure all critical processes are well-documented and accessible.
   - **Encourage Adherence:** Promote a culture where following and improving systems is valued.

4. **Implement Effective Measurement**
   - **Select Relevant KPIs:** Identify key metrics that align with your strategic goals.
   - **Create Dashboards:** Develop visual tools for real-time monitoring and decision-making.

5. **Cultivate Strong Relationships**
   - **Engage Stakeholders:** Regularly connect with clients, vendors, and partners to strengthen ties.

- **Prioritize Employee Relations:** Create initiatives that enhance employee satisfaction and retention.

6. **Enhance Communication**
   - **Promote Transparency:** Share successes, challenges, and updates openly.
   - **Encourage Dialogue:** Establish forums for feedback and collaboration at all levels.

7. **Drive Innovation**
   - **Allocate Resources:** Dedicate time and budget to research and development.
   - **Celebrate Creativity:** Recognize and reward innovative ideas and risk-taking.

Leading by Example and Inspiring Teams

Being a successful leader is more than just making decisions or managing resources—it's about setting a standard that others want to follow. Your actions, words, and mindset create a ripple effect that influences your team far beyond what any policy or memo ever could. If you want your team to be innovative, purposeful, and committed, you have to show them what that looks like in action. Leadership isn't a title; it's a responsibility. And the most powerful way to inspire others is by demonstrating the very qualities and behaviors you expect from them every day. This section dives into what it truly means to lead by example and how your own actions can shape a culture of success.

- **Be the Role Model:**
  - **Embody the Values:** Live out the organization's core values in your daily actions.
  - **Demonstrate Commitment:** Show unwavering dedication to The Essential Elements.

- **Communicate Vision with Passion:**
  - **Inspire Through Storytelling:** Share anecdotes that illustrate the Purpose and impact.
  - **Maintain Enthusiasm:** Your energy can be contagious—in a good way!

- **Empower Others:**
  - **Delegate Authority:** Trust your team with responsibilities and decision-making power.
  - **Provide Support:** Offer guidance and resources to help them succeed.

- **Foster a Positive Culture:**
  - **Encourage Collaboration:** Break down silos and promote cross-functional teamwork.
  - **Recognize Achievements:** Celebrate successes, both big and small, like it's everyone's birthday.

FOR ENTREPRENEURS AND STARTUPS

As an entrepreneur, you know that turning a dream into a reality means balancing vision with action and creativity with execution. While it's easy to get caught up in the excitement of launching new products or securing that next big investment, building a business that truly stands the test of time requires more than a brilliant idea. It demands a strong foundation rooted in The Essential Elements. Right now, you're at a critical stage where every decision you make can set the trajectory for years to come. Think of this as your opportunity to build your organization's DNA—one that's purpose-driven, customer-centric, and ready to scale.

The beauty of being a startup is that you have the freedom to shape your company culture, define your systems, and establish clear strategies from day one. You're not bogged down by legacy processes or the weight of "how things have always been done." This is your blank slate, where you can weave The Essential Elements into the very fabric of your business. Whether it's defining your Purpose, attracting a stellar Team, or setting up streamlined Systems, the groundwork you lay today will either support rapid growth or crack under pressure when challenges arise.

This section is packed with practical, straightforward advice to help you navigate the unique challenges of early-stage business building. By thoughtfully applying these elements from the outset, you'll create a business that's not just agile and innovative, but also purpose-driven and structured for long-term success. Because the goal isn't just to launch—it's to build something enduring.

So let's set you up with the strategies and tools to turn your startup into a powerhouse that can thrive, scale, and, ultimately, leave a lasting impact in your industry.

Integrating the Elements from the Outset

1. **Define Your Purpose Early**
   - **Start with Why:** Clearly articulate the mission and vision before diving into the 'what' and 'how.'
   - **Align Your Team:** Even if it's just you and your dog (who makes an excellent Chief Morale Officer), ensure everyone understands and embraces the Purpose.

2. **Assemble the Right Team**
   - **Hire for Cultural Fit:** Skills are essential, but shared values are crucial for a cohesive startup culture.
   - **Diversify Skills:** Build a team with complementary strengths to cover all bases.

3. **Establish Systems Early On**
   - **Document as You Go:** Create processes even when the team is small to set the foundation for scalability.
   - **Stay Flexible:** Keep systems adaptable to accommodate rapid growth and change.

4. **Embrace Measurement**
    - **Set Metrics that Matter:** Focus on key indicators like customer acquisition cost, burn rate, and user engagement.
    - **Iterate Based on Data:** Use analytics to inform pivots and improvements.

5. **Build Relationships**
    - **Network Relentlessly:** Connect with mentors, investors, potential partners, and customers.
    - **Provide Value:** Offer insights or assistance without expecting immediate returns.

6. **Communicate Clearly**
    - **Pitch Perfectly:** Hone your ability to articulate your vision succinctly to different audiences.
    - **Stay Transparent:** Keep your team informed to build trust and commitment.

7. **Foster an Innovative Mindset**
    - **Encourage Experimentation:** Create a safe space for testing ideas without fear of failure.
    - **Stay Curious:** Continuously explore industry trends and emerging technologies.

Leveraging Them for Sustainable Growth

Establishing a startup is one thing; growing it into a sustainable, thriving business is another challenge entirely. The Essential Elements are more than just a blueprint for getting started—they're your playbook for building an organization that can adapt, evolve, and expand without losing its foundation. To achieve sustainable growth, you need to think beyond short-term wins and focus on creating scalable processes, nurturing a resilient team, and staying true to your core Purpose as you expand. This section will show you how to leverage each element to fuel long-term success, helping you transform your startup from a promising venture into an enduring, profitable enterprise.

- **Focus on Sustainable Practices:**
    - **Long-Term Vision:** Balance immediate needs with future goals to avoid burnout and build longevity.
    - **Ethical Operations:** Prioritize integrity and social responsibility from day one.

- **Adapt and Evolve:**
    - **Stay Agile:** Be prepared to pivot based on market feedback and evolving circumstances.
    - **Learn from Others:** Study both successful and failed startups to glean valuable lessons.

- **Build a Strong Brand:**
    - **Consistent Messaging:** Align all communications with your core values and Purpose.
    - **Engage Your Audience:** Foster a community around your brand through authentic interactions.

| FOR INDIVIDUALS AT ANY LEVEL

No matter where you are in the organizational hierarchy—whether you're leading a team, managing projects, or contributing as a dedicated team member—you have the power to shape the success of your company. You don't need a fancy title or a corner office to make an impact. True influence comes from embodying the values that drive success and consistently taking actions that reflect The Essential Elements. When you invest in your own growth and strive to elevate those around you, you become a catalyst for positive change, creating ripples that spread throughout the organization.

While you may not have direct control over the company's Purpose, Strategy, or Systems, you can play a vital role in strengthening the culture, improving Communication, and building stronger Relationships within your sphere of influence. By mastering these elements on a personal level, you can lead by example, inspire your peers, and contribute to a more engaged and cohesive environment. When others see you aligning your actions with these principles, it encourages them to do the same, reinforcing a shared commitment to excellence.

This section is filled with practical tips and strategies designed to empower you—no matter your position—to become a driving force for progress. From refining your personal Communication skills to nurturing valuable

Relationships and embracing a mindset of continuous improvement, you'll learn how to apply The Essential Elements in ways that not only elevate your performance but also contribute to the success of the entire organization. After all, meaningful change often starts with a single individual choosing to make a difference. Why not let that person be you?

Personal Development Through Embracing the Elements

1. **Clarify Your Personal Purpose**
   - **Self-Reflection:** Identify your passions, strengths, and what brings you fulfillment.
   - **Set Goals:** Align your career objectives with your personal Purpose.

2. **Enhance Your Skills**
   - **Continuous Learning:** Pursue training, certifications, or education to build expertise.
   - **Seek Feedback:** Regularly ask for input to identify areas for improvement.

3. **Build Your Network**
   - **Cultivate Relationships:** Connect with colleagues, mentors, and industry peers.
   - **Offer Value:** Share knowledge and support others in their endeavors.

4. **Communicate Effectively**
    - **Practice Active Listening:** Understand before seeking to be understood.
    - **Improve Presentation Skills:** Enhance your ability to convey ideas clearly and persuasively.

5. **Embrace Innovation**
    - **Stay Inquisitive:** Keep up with industry trends and be open to new ideas.
    - **Take Initiative:** Propose improvements or novel solutions within your role.

Contributing to a Culture of Excellence

Creating a culture of excellence isn't reserved for those at the top—it's something that every individual can help shape and sustain through their daily actions and attitudes. Excellence is more than just doing your job well; it's about striving for continuous improvement, encouraging others to bring their best, and fostering an environment where high standards are the norm. Whether it's consistently delivering quality work, providing constructive feedback, or simply modeling positive behaviors, your efforts set the tone for those around you. This section will explore how you can contribute to building a culture where people feel empowered, engaged, and committed to achieving outstanding results together.

- **Lead from Where You Are:**
  - **Be Proactive:** Don't wait for permission to make positive changes.
  - **Demonstrate Integrity:** Uphold ethical standards and encourage others to do the same.

- **Foster Collaboration:**
  - **Share Knowledge:** Help teammates by sharing insights and resources.
  - **Encourage Diversity of Thought:** Welcome different perspectives to enrich discussions.

- **Support Organizational Goals:**
  - **Align Efforts:** Ensure your work contributes to the organization's Purpose and objectives.
  - **Champion the Elements:** Advocate for the implementation of The Essential Elements.

- **Recognize and Celebrate:**
  - **Acknowledge Others:** Celebrate colleagues' achievements and contributions.
  - **Promote Positivity:** Contribute to a supportive and motivating work environment.

FINAL THOUGHTS: TURNING POSSIBILITY INTO REALITY

The Essential Elements isn't a mystical incantation or a secret handshake reserved for the elite. It's a practical framework accessible to anyone willing to embrace it. By taking action, you transform potential into performance, and dreams into achievements.

Remember:

- **Start Small:** You don't have to overhaul everything overnight. Begin with one factor and build momentum.
- **Stay Committed:** Change takes time and perseverance. Keep pushing forward, even when challenges arise.
- **Inspire Others:** Your actions can influence and motivate those around you, creating a ripple effect of positive change.

As you embark on this journey, keep in mind that success is not a solo endeavor. Whether you're leading an organization, launching a startup, or contributing within a team, collaboration amplifies impact.

So, step boldly into action. The roadmap is laid out, the destination is clear, and the only thing left is to begin. As the saying goes, "The best time to plant a tree was 20 years ago. The second-best time is now."

Your future awaits—let's make it extraordinary!

CONCLUSION

It's funny how life can take you from being homeless behind a diner in a map-dot of a town to discussing business strategies in boardrooms with views so high you can almost see yesterday. If someone had told 15-year-old me, while I was splitting a stale burger bun with my whiskered pals behind a dumpster, that I'd one day be writing a book about the secrets of organizational success, I'd have handed them the other half of that bun and said, "Buddy, you need this more than I do."

But here we are, at the end of this journey together—a journey that started with a teenager determined to change his circumstances and evolved into a lifelong quest to understand what makes some organizations soar like eagles while others flop around like penguins attempting flight.

The Essential Elements isn't some mystical elixir concocted in the secret labs of Fortune 500 companies.

It's a distillation of common-sense principles that, when applied thoughtfully, can transform not just businesses but the lives of everyone involved. We've explored **Purpose**, the North Star that guides every decision; **Team**, the ensemble cast that brings the script to life; **Systems**, the backbone that keeps everything upright even when the winds of chaos blow; **Measurement**, the gauges and dials that prevent you from flying blind; **Relationships**, the glue that holds the human elements together; **Communication**, the language that turns ideas into action; and **Innovation**, the spark that ignites progress and keeps stagnation at bay.

Looking back, I realize that these elements were at play even during my toughest times. My **Purpose** was survival first, then creating a better future. My **Team** consisted of anyone willing to lend a hand or share a word of encouragement. The **Systems** were the routines that kept me safe, the **Measurements** were the mental notes of what worked and what didn't, and the **Relationships** included the kind souls who offered help when I needed it most. **Communication** came in the form of understanding unspoken rules and signals, and **Innovation** was figuring out how to turn limited resources into opportunities.

Fast forward to my corporate adventures, and these elements became more sophisticated but no less essential. I remember joining a startup that had all the makings of the next big thing—a product that could revolutionize the industry, investors with pockets deeper than philosophical questions at 2 a.m., and a team of geniuses who could probably solve a Rubik's Cube blindfolded while reciting the periodic table backwards. But they lacked a clear **Purpose**. Meetings were like ships passing in the night, each steering toward a different lighthouse. It was like watching a group of virtuoso musicians each playing a different song; the talent was there, but the harmony was missing.

Contrast that with another company where I consulted. They made something as unglamorous as industrial adhesives. Not exactly the stuff that gets you a million followers on social media. But they had their act together. Their **Purpose** was clear: "To bond the world together, one solution at a time." Their **Team** was engaged and knew exactly how their roles contributed to the bigger picture. They had **Systems** in place that made operations smoother than a freshly ironed silk shirt. **Measurements** were meticulously tracked, **Relationships** with clients and suppliers were nurtured like prized roses, **Communication** was open and effective, and **Innovation** was encouraged even in something as seemingly mundane as glue.

The result? They dominated their market niche, had enviable employee retention rates, and received thank-you letters from clients who appreciated their commitment—yes, people were writing love letters about glue.

So what's the takeaway here? Whether you're trying to claw your way out of homelessness or steering a multinational corporation, the principles remain strikingly similar. The Essential Elements isn't reserved for the elite or those with Ivy League degrees and corner offices. It's for anyone and everyone who dares to strive for something better.

Now, I won't pretend that applying these elements is as easy as ordering a pizza (and even that can get complicated—thin crust or deep dish?). It requires effort, introspection, and sometimes making tough decisions that feel about as pleasant as a root canal without anesthesia. But the rewards? They're worth every ounce of sweat and every moment of doubt.

Imagine leading an organization where everyone understands the **Purpose** and is genuinely excited about it. Picture a **Team** that's not just clocking in hours but is deeply invested in mutual success. Envision **Systems** that streamline operations so efficiently that you have time to focus on growth rather than putting out fires. Think about having real-time **Measurements** that inform your decisions, **Relationships** that open doors you didn't even know existed, **Communication** that eliminates misunderstandings, and an environment where **Innovation** isn't a buzzword but a daily practice.

Does it sound like a utopia? Perhaps. But it's more attainable than you might think.

So here's my challenge to you: **Take decisive action**. Don't let this book become another addition to the "I'll get to it someday" pile, which, let's be honest, is starting to resemble the leaning tower of Pisa. Start today. Assess where you stand with each of the seven elements. Be brutally honest—this isn't the time for sugarcoating. Identify one small step for each factor that you can implement immediately. It doesn't have to be monumental; even a journey of a thousand miles begins with a single step, or so the saying goes.

Remember, change doesn't happen by accident. It happens by choice. By choosing to act, you're not just improving your organization; you're setting in motion a ripple effect that can positively impact everyone connected to it—employees, customers, suppliers, and maybe even that kid who's watching from the sidelines, wondering how to change his own circumstances.

The potential for positive change and success is immense. And while there are no guarantees in life—except maybe death, taxes, and the disappointment of a vending machine eating your dollar—the odds are decidedly in your favor when you apply The Essential Elements.

I am not the smartest guy in the world, but what I do know is that if a homeless teenager can climb out of despair armed with nothing but determination and a penchant for organizing chaos, then you, with all the resources at your disposal, can certainly transform your organization and perhaps even leave a legacy that makes the world just a little bit better.

So go ahead—dive in, embrace the elements, and let's see where this journey takes you. The road ahead is open, the possibilities are vast, and the only thing left to do is take that first step.

And remember, I'm here whenever you need support—whether it's to celebrate your victories, help you navigate a tough decision, or simply offer encouragement when the road feels challenging. We all need support now and then...and at least I don't have a long tail and beady eyes.

www.ingramcontent.com/pod-product-compliance
Lightning Source LLC
Chambersburg PA
CBHW060849170526
45158CB00001B/288